Contents

Staff Training and Special Educational Needs

Edited by
Graham Upton

David Fulton Publishers

David Fulton Publishers Ltd
2 Barbon Close, London WC1N 3JX

First published in Great Britain by
David Fulton Publishers 1991,

British Library Cataloguing in Publication Data

Staff training and special education needs.
  1. Teaching, Professional education
  I. Upton, Graham *1944–*
371.907

  ISBN 1-85346-172-5

Typeset by Chapterhouse, Formby
Printed in Great Britain by
Biddles Ltd. Guildford

CHAPTER 1

Introduction: Issues and Trends in Staff Training

Graham Upton

The chapters which constitute this book are based on papers delivered at the International Special Education Congress held in Cardiff in the summer of 1990. At this conference staff training was one of the central themes on which the call for papers was based. The decision to make staff training a major focus of the congress was a bold move on the part of the organisers, for while many appear to recognise the importance of specialised staff training in relation to special educational needs, few have written about it or spoken about it at national and international conferences.

In 1989, for example, when the international special education conference was held in Vancouver only a handful of papers addressed training issues. Similarly, a survey of the literature quickly reveals that it is a relatively ignored topic both in general literature and research. Specialist staff training as a topic rarely features in journals, rarely forms the basis of research and constitutes the content of very few books indeed. Why this should be the case is not clear, although training issues clearly do not have the immediate relevance which curriculum issues have for the teacher or which service delivery has for the administrator; staff training lacks the colour and immediate appeal of more practically oriented issues. And yet, in many ways specialist staff training is central to the definition of special education as 'special'. If special education is truly special then it must surely necessitate special training. If special training is not essential, in what sense is special education special?

1

In the present chapter an attempt has been made to explore this apparent enigma by raising basic questions about staff training and, in so doing, provide a framework for the other contributions. More specifically, the intention is to:

(a) further elucidate this indifference to staff training and to explore reasons for its relatively low status as a topic for debate,
(b) explore some of the key issues affecting the delivery of training, and
(c) speculate about the importance of specialist training in the process of educational development.

The importance of training

On a number of occasions recently, groups of teachers, administrators and others involved in the field of special education have been asked by the present author to indicate how important they consider training to be in determining the efficacy of special educational provision. More particularly, they have been asked to respond to the following question: 'How important to the efficacy of special educational provision do you consider specialised teacher training to be?'.

Given the opportunity to respond in terms of it being, not important/moderately important/important/very important/extremely important, responses have overwhelmingly favoured its rating as either very important or extremely important.

In contrast to such assertions of its importance, specialist training is far from the norm. Statistical information in this area is not easy to find but the following data help to illustrate the status which is accorded to specialist training in a number of countries.

(1) In the United Kingdom in 1984, 'less than 30% of the qualified teachers in special schools have a recognised additional qualification specifically related to special educational needs' (Advisory Committee on the Supply and Education of Teachers, 1984).

(2) In Australia, Andrews (1983) reported that a survey had revealed that 64 per cent of the special school teachers claimed to have undertaken some form of special educational training but one third of these had received the training as part of their pre-service education.

(3) In the United States of America, in spite of the certification system designed to ensure that special needs teachers have appropriate qualifications, Huebner and Strumwasser (1987) found in relation to the blind and visually impaired that:

   – 45 states required/offered specific certification for teachers of blind and visually impaired children, while five did not.

- 25 states offered emergency registration for one year and one state offered emergency registration for five years to teachers who were deficient in certain areas of study required for certification.
- 16 states allowed uncertified teachers to work with blind and visually impaired children.

(4) In Japan, in spite of the widespread availability of specialist training courses, 'A normal licence or temporary licence for primary and junior high school teaching will be sufficient to teach special classes' (National Institute of Special Education, 1986).

(5) In Zimbabwe, Kabzems (1989) reported that in 1987 the numbers of trained and untrained teachers working in special classes were as follows:

	Trained	Untrained	Total
Visual impairment	56	29	85
Hearing impairment	25	98	128
Mental handicap	6	69	75
Total	87	196	283

In sum, the untrained outnumbered the trained.

(6) In many countries staff training frequently lags way behind actual provision. Thus,
- In Britain special schools for the blind were established in the early 19th Century. The first university training course started in 1954.
- In Algeria, Boucebi and Brau (1981) refer to the 'extreme shortage of qualified staff' available to work within existing provision for the mentally handicapped.
- In Indonesia, Carpenter (1987) noted the existence of a specialist training course only on the Island of Java and the lack of trained teachers elsewhere.

It is clearly not possible to draw firm conclusions on the basis of personal responses to the question noted above, or on the snippets of information which have been listed. However, in the absence of more representative data, we are nonetheless faced with a fundamental question about training, viz: 'Is special education training really necessary'?

It is expensive, particularly in the context of competing demands on educational budgets, and especially in the contexts of stringency which prevail in developing countries. Furthermore, if special schools/classes can function without specially trained staff, as is apparent from the information cited above, then is it needed at all?

While the teachers and administrators cited above may well believe in its value and importance, it is difficult to provide hard evidence to support such feelings. A search of the literature, for example, produces virtually no research data which demonstrate the benefits of training. In Britain, the official report on teacher training and special educational needs to which reference was made above (Advisory Committee on the Supply and Education of Teachers, 1984) based its conclusion on unsubstantiated assertions about its importance. At no point did it have evidence before it which demonstrated the efficacy of specialist training.

While the majority of special educators may assert that special training is necessary if special education is to be effective it is important to recognise that they generally do so on the basis of beliefs and a priori assumptions about its value. Clearly there is a need for research to investigate the real significance of training. While it would be distressing if such research showed specialist training to be of little value, it is possible that an edifice has been erected for which there is no practical justification.

Issues affecting delivery of training

A fundamental, but often ignored issue underlying the provision of specialist training is the relationship between the nature of special educational provision and training. Working, as most special educators do, within the confines of a national educational system it is easy to overlook the extent to which the meaning of special education has become so diverse. The international conference from which the papers in this book were drawn was helpful in identifying this issue. Even a casual examination of the papers which addressed the provision of special education in developing countries drew immediate attention to the extent of the differences which exist in the definition of special educational needs.

In many developing countries concepts of disability and handicap still play a fundamental role in the definition of special educational needs while in countries such as Britain they now play a relatively small part in the understanding of special needs. Categorical concepts have come to be seen negatively and in terms of a deficit model of functioning and have been almost universally replaced by more positive constructions of educational need. In countries such as Britain the concept of special education has been broadened to cater for a much larger group of children and young people and to focus on educational needs irrespective of the handicap or disability. At the same time much effort has been concentrated on making provision for these children, where possible, in ordinary schools. *Integration* has become the catchword.

The implications which these changes have for training are far reaching and in some ways render international dialogue about training difficult. In countries where the concept of special needs has been extended, special attention has to be given to training a very much larger group of people to be able to recognise and cater for children with special educational needs and in consequence attention has begun to shift from specialist training to more generic training.

Pre-service training

Regardless of the educational system in which one is working, a primary concern in initial training is to familiarise trainees with the nature of special educational needs and to help them develop ways of identifying and coping adequately with those needs. In Britain, an attempt has been made to ensure that this happens by introducing accreditation requirements which demand that courses should prepare students for teaching the full range of pupils and the diversity of ability, behaviour, social background and ethnic and cultural origin they are likely to encounter among pupils in ordinary schools. More specifically, the accreditation requirements state that on completion of their course students should have developed:

(i) an understanding of the different ways in which pupils develop and learn and the ways in which pupils' work can be planned to secure clear progression,

(ii) the capacity to use a range of teaching methods appropriate to the different abilities and other needs of pupils and organise their work accordingly,

(iii) the capacity to identify gifted pupils and pupils with special educational needs or with learning difficulties, and to understand ways in which the potential of such pupils can be developed,

(iv) skills in the evaluation of pupil performance,

(v) the capacity to guard against pre-conceptions based on the race, gender or other attributes of pupils.

Such intentions are shared by special educators in many countries, developed and developing. Whether they are successful in achieving these aims is not clear. Once again hard evidence is lacking but, as Keith Bovair suggests in his chapter in this book, while requirement three is commonly met, the others are less frequently addressed satisfactorily. This may be changing (see, for example, Boardman, 1982, Ramasut, 1989). It is possible that this may be a largely British phenomenon *but* in the present author's experience, at least, subject specialists who have experience and expertise in the teaching of their subject to children with special educational needs are very rare creatures indeed. *And yet*, the success of integration/mainstreaming depends on the preparedness of ordinary classroom teachers, not only to recognise, but also to meet, special needs. In this context it is apparent that training is lagging behind practice.

Another concern for those involved in initial training is to prepare teachers to work in the cultural context of which they are part. This is relevant to both ordinary and special educational training and is particularly important in relation to the multicultural issues which increasingly face developed and industrialised nations. The chapter in this volume by Victoria Graf draws attention to this issue and provides a model on which others may wish to base more positive attempts to cater for it within their courses.

Further professional development

In relation to the further professional development of teachers the changed conceptualisation of special education has brought with it problems of what we should do in specialist training and at the same time created the need for a whole range of new demands for in-service training.

Specialist courses

The movements towards integration/mainstreaming and the growing emphasis on the educational needs of special children has raised doubts about the pattern and content of specialist training courses. In spite of a growing recognition that the educational and social needs of different groups of special needs children overlap in many ways, few attempts have been made to identify those aspects of training which could be regarded as non-categorical or generic and those which are clearly category specific.

In the United States Newhouse (1981) reported that: '70 or more institutions of higher education across our nation now offer generic programs in special education. However, the majority continue to tie their programs to an existing certification area'.

While the pattern reported by Newhouse may have altered since

1981, Huebner and Strumwasser (1987) stress 'The need for national standards for areas of competence that are required by state certification boards and the preparation programs of colleges and universities'.

Once again, the absence of documented evidence allows generalisation on the basis of personal experience and this suggests that few (if any) countries have progressed this far. This can be seen as further evidence of less than full support for the importance of training.

New demands

As noted above, changing concepts of special education have also brought with them the need for the in-service education of a much larger group of teachers and other workers who may come into contact with special needs children as a result of integration/mainstreaming. There has also been a recognition of the need for administrators and those who hold positions of power within institutions and within educational authorities to be trained in order that they may sponsor and effect institutional change to cater most effectively for these needs.

Attempts to provide for this former group of workers have been varied and often innovative. Ainscow and Muncey (1983) describe a comprehensive training programme for an entire English Local Education Authority based on a self-contained multi-media package of the type sometimes referred to as a mini-course. Wolf (1981) describes an individualised needs-based training programme designed to cater for state-wide needs in Alaska, made particularly difficult by its uneven geographical distribution of resources and personnel.

Equally, the need to train 'untrained' support staff such as classroom assistants has been increasingly recognised, as is indicated in this volume in the chapter by Maggie Balshaw. In contrast, attempts to provide training for those who manage the system have been infrequent and inadequate.

The extension of special education

The recognition that special education needs to extend above and below the conventional ages of school attendance has focused attention on the need for extended training emphases. The popularity of pre-school intervention which came about in the mid-1960s and early 1970s served to focus attention on training for the early years but the needs of young people and adults beyond the level of ordinary schooling have only just begun to be addressed, as is pointed out by David Hutchinson in his chapter on further education training in Britain.

Cooperation with parents/other professionals

The benefits which may accrue from cooperation between teachers and parents and other professionals is widely recognised as being relevant to all ages and stages of education and to all children, but it does have particular relevance to the education of children with special educational needs. However, a search for documented material about the response of training programmes to this need reveals few attempts by trainers to incorporate such developments into their thinking. A review of the literature reveals little relevant material although an example of such interest is reflected in the work of Haron and Harris (1982) who provide a training manual for working with other professional groups and parents. The chapter in this volume by Rachel David and Beryl Smith outlines an innovative approach to fostering collaboration between professional groups by incorporating collaboration into the initial training courses of speech therapists and teachers.

Modes of delivery

A lack of money to support further professional development for large numbers of teachers, together with the changing conceptualisation of special education to which reference has been made above, has highlighted a need to look seriously at the patterns of training which currently exist and the ways in which we attempt to deliver training. When one does this it becomes clear that our present forms of training are in many instances out of line with changes in provision and have already demonstrated their unsuitability to meet training needs. With regard to the figures referred to earlier in this chapter, it could be argued that all too often our response to the huge gap which exists between trained staff and total staff numbers has been ostrich-like: we have buried our head in the sand. We have blamed governments for lack of financial support to enable all teachers to be trained and persevered with a demand for what we see as essential/minimum levels of training. An alternative would be to question the realism of our assumptions about training and to develop a more coherent framework for training which is in line with the realities of inadequate finances and the *competing* demands of basic training in many countries.

This suggests that there is a need to look seriously at the way in which training is delivered. In many countries it is assumed that the training that is required must be of a long duration – 1 to 2 years or the equivalent on a part-time basis. It is also commonly assumed that such courses should be based on institutions of higher education, such as universities and colleges. Such assertions may not be realistic or necessarily appropriate.

A framework for planning school-focused post-experience training is outlined in this volume in the chapter by Mel Myers and Roger Solomon. Their approach focuses on the identification of needs within a system (for example, a school) and requires that training is directly geared to meet those needs. Alternative training models are suggested elsewhere in this book by Richard Freeze and Winston Rampaul who promote the value of a consultative approach to improving classroom teaching skills, and Gerda Hanko who introduces a problem-solving approach to in-school training. Equally interesting in the area of post-experience training, is the chapter by Heather Mason and Carol Miller which looks at the potential of distance learning as a solution to the provision of specialised teacher training while Alan Peacock and Christina Tilstone outline the benefits of IT-INSET for both initial and post-experience training.

Disappointingly, however, few people at the international conference addressed the potential of new and micro technology. This could revolutionise information exchange and transmission in many countries and, as Roy McConkey and Alice Bradley point out in their chapter in this book, could constitute a cost-effective and efficient means of providing training even in conditions of economic stringency in developing countries.

But perhaps most important is the growing awareness of many of the value of on-the-job training; training that is directly related to, and grows out of, actual experience. Teacher appraisal, as Ian Petrie and Kath Williams point out, has great potential for identifying the training needs of individual teachers and ensuring that training is provided which is relevant to those needs and in accord with the interests and overall needs of the school. Christine O'Hanlon, in advocating the benefits of action research in post-experience training, describes a way in which institutions of higher education have developed innovative approaches to course delivery which facilitate teachers' exploration of their own work experience. However, a more typical response, perhaps, to meet this desire for training to be directly related to teachers' experience has been the move away from institutionally-based courses to more flexible means of disseminating ideas and materials. This trend is already well under way in many countries and is reflected in the chapter in this volume by Martyn Rouse and Maggie Balshaw which addresses collaborative working between an institution of higher education and a Local Education Authority. While these represent very different responses to the need for change, these papers all report school-based training projects which challenge tradition and promulgate innovatory forms of training.

Implications for development

The value of an international conference is that it brings together people from a broad geographical spectrum. There are clearly great benefits to be gained from the exchange of information which takes place in such a forum. However, there is the danger in such an exchange that the practices of the more developed world come to be seen as models which others should emulate. The differences which were noted above as existing between countries in relation to the concept of special education should however alert us all to the dangers of educational imperialism. As teacher educators it is important to recognise that training should be related directly to its context. As Venta Kabzems argues in her chapter in this volume, this has special implications for countries whose educational systems are at a basic stage of development.

Ethnocentricity characterises the way in which we all view the world and views on teacher education are no exception. Carpenter (1987) provides an example of this when he introduces his paper on special education in Indonesia as follows:

> With occasional exceptions, special education services and teacher preparation seem to be a North American enterprise. There is the important influence of the Scandinavian approach to serving people who are mentally retarded; there was the International Conference of the Council for Exceptional Children in Scotland in 1978; and most university libraries subscribe to at least a few British education journals. But for the most part, our field relies on North American networks, conferences, journals and programs for information about developments in special education, policy, research, teacher education, and service delivery (p. 37).

To a British special educator such a statement is astonishing, to say the least, but typifies the way in which our views are determined often by very limited experience and understanding. The extent to which such limited views are often accepted by, or imposed upon, others is highlighted in many developing countries where special education training has been modelled on that of western countries often with virtually no change to make it meaningful in the local context. This is well illustrated by reference to a course outline for a specialist course for teachers of the deaf which is provided in one of the least developed educational systems in Africa. The content is set out as follows:

1 CHILD DEVELOPMENT
    a. Linguistic development in relation to mental growth.
    b. Social and emotional development.
    c. Learning.
    d. Assessments of abilities and attainments.
    e. Physical growth.

2 PSYCHOLOGY OF DEAFNESS
    a. Nature and extent of deafness.
    b. Deafness and psychological processes.
    c. Language and speech, speech reading, reading, writing.
    d. Other handicaps and learning disabilities.

3 SPEECH AND AUDITORY TRAINING, INCLUDING:
    a. Development and function of speech as a means of communication.
    b. The development in deaf children of the capacity to understand speech and to talk.
    c. Phonetics.
    d. Methods of teaching speech to deaf children.

4 AUDIOLOGY
    a. Elementary physics of sound, including room acoustics.
    b. Physics of speech and hearing.
    c. Measurement of hearing.
    d. Design, performance and use of hearing-aids, audio-meters, and other electronic equipment used in deaf education.
    e. Anatomy, pathology of the ear and physiology of speech and hearing.
    f. Causes of deafness.

5 CURRICULUM AND METHODS OF TEACHING
   a. – in schools for the deaf
      – in schools for partially-hearing children.
      – at different stages: nursery/infant/junior/secondary
      – for children with other handicaps, associated with deafness.
   b. Methods of linguistic teaching.
   c. Teaching of reading.
   d. Subjects: English, mathematics, geography, history, science, spiritual and moral development.
   e. The use of visual aids in schools for the deaf. Production of teaching aids, adapted for teaching of the deaf.

6 PRACTICAL WORK IN TEACHING
   a. School practice and demonstrations.
   b. School visits.
   c. Practical work with deaf and partially deaf children.

Academically sound though this outline may be, it lacks any reference to the educational system in which it is based. No account, for example, is taken of the fact that the resources which are available to teachers are rudimentary and that knowledge of electronic devices will be of little value to teachers who for the most part work in areas where the supply of electricity is sporadic and unreliable and where maintenance for even the simplest of modern technology is non-existent.

At the same time, assumptions about the value of ideas and materials produced in developed countries are being challenged increasingly by workers in less developed areas. Boucebi and Brau (1981) for example, argue that:

> In the countries of the Third World, the urgency and the immensity of the need for staff trained in the care of the mentally handicapped calls for the formulation of training programmes which can be rapidly and realistically implemented, but which can still be integrated into medium and long-term programmes. These programmes should not be modelled on the sophisticated and expensive techniques and structures developed in the industrialised countries, which are ill-suited to local socio-cultural conditions (p. 105).

This need for training to reflect the local context as well as being responsive to the latest thinking about special educational needs is central to the chapter in this book by Mel Ainscow. This describes the development of a training programme which arises out of 'western' experience but which, through a process of collaborative development and evaluation, is being made meaningful for use within the context of educational development.

Conclusion

Where do these thoughts leave us? Clearly every answer to that question will depend upon the respondent's involvement in training and the context in which he or she works – national and local. Nonetheless, some general points commend themselves for consideration:

(1) There is a need for us to look more critically at our present provision for special educational training. We must ask, why is it like it is? Is it the result of historical accident or is it planned to meet current needs?
(2) There is a need to consider what current training needs are and to think through how training programmes could be devised to meet those needs more effectively.
(3) In undertaking these tasks it is important to bear in mind
    (a) the need for training to be embedded in its educational context,
    (b) the need for a coherent training programme which takes into account the needs of all – specialists and generalists, classroom teachers and school administrators, and which allows continued professional development,
    (c) the need for a flexible programme which is responsive to changing patterns of provision and priorities in special education,
    (d) the overriding need to be realistic in such planning and to relate such proposals to financial exigencies and other pressures within educational systems.

References

Advisory Committee on the Supply and Education of Teachers (1984) *Teacher Training and Special Educational Needs*. London: DES.
Ainscow, M. and Muncey, J. (1983) 'Learning difficulties in the primary school: an in-service training intitiative', *Remedial Education*, **18**, 116–24.
Andrews, R. J. (1983) 'Issues in the professional preparation of special education teachers: An Australian overview', *The Exceptional Child*, **30**, 2, 101–10.
Boardman, D. (1982) *Geography with Slow Learners*. Sheffield: Geographical Association.
Boucebi, M. and Brau, M. T. (1981) 'Training specialised staff for the mentally handicapped', *Assignment Children*, **53/54**, 105–14.

Carpenter, R. L. (1987) 'Special education teacher preparation and service delivery in a developing country: Indonesia', *Teacher Education and Special Education* **10**, 1, 37–43.

Haron, T. E. and Harris, K. C. (1982) *The Educational Consultant*. Boston: Allyn and Bacon.

Huebner, K. M. and Strumwasser, K. P. (1987) 'State certification of teachers of blind and visually impaired students: Report of a national study', *Journal of Visual Impairment and Blindness*, **81**, 6, 244–50.

Kabzems, V. (1989) 'Special Education in Zimbabwe'. Paper delivered at the International Conference on Special Education held at The University of British Columbia, April 1989.

National Institute for Special Education (1986) *Special Education in Japan*. Yokosuka, Japan: NISE.

Newhouse, J. (1981) 'A cross-disciplinary special education preparation program', *Journal of Teacher Education*, **32**, 4, 38–41.

Ramasut, A. (Ed.) (1989) *Special Educational Needs: The Whole School Approach*. London: Falmer Press.

Wolf, S. (1981) 'The Alaska Special Education In-Service Training Centre', *Journal of Staff Development*, **2**, 2, 6–18.

CHAPTER 2

Preparing Special Education Needs Teachers For a Multicultural Society

Victoria L. Graf

In the United States, the majority of university-based special education courses have been preparing White monolingual English-speaking teachers to work with White pupils who also speak English. However, due to demographic changes, teacher education is now being asked to prepare these teachers to function in a multicultural and multilingual society. This chapter describes the development and evaluation of a special education teacher education program at Loyola Marymount University in Los Angeles, California, which has attempted to meet the needs of a culturally and linguistically diverse (CLD) population.

Background

Demographics

The demographic makeup of many industrialised nations is changing and more and more countries are experiencing change in the cultural and linguistic diversity of the students who are in school. For example, the United States is becoming less White (Yates, 1988). By the year 2000, it is projected that one of every three individuals will be either Asian, African-American or Hispanic. Hispanics are the fastest growing population with a projected increase from 7 per cent of the population in 1986 to 19 per cent by the year 2080 (Reich, in Yates, 1988). In California, one of the largest states in the United States, White pupils have already been replaced as the majority group in the general school pupulation by a combination of Asian, Pacific Islanders, African-Americans, Hispanic and other smaller ethnic groups. The California State Department of Education which collects racial and ethnic data on public school students and staff reported the following information from the 1990 report which illustrates the current demographics in California: 'Of the almost four and three-quarter million students enrolled in the public schools, 52.9 per cent were reported as being members of racial/ethnic groups other than white' (California State Department of Education, 1990).

In addition, California receives a larger than proportional influx of immigrants from various countries. According to California Tomorrow (1988), the proportion of immigrant students in the state's public schools has more than doubled to 16 per cent since 1978 and is projected to grow by 5 to 7 per cent a year over the next decade.

With respect to the special education population in California, a count of students with special education needs in 1989 reported that out of a total of 472,586 students, 47.77 per cent were of ethnicities other than White. The following is a breakdown by ethnic group, according to the California State Department of Education (1990):

Ethnic Group	Per cent
African-American	11.79
Asian	3.33
Filipino	0.32
Hispanic	30.72
Native American	0.73
Pacific Islander	0.32

In addition to the ethnic background of the pupils, another important issue is their mother tongue and language proficiency. For example, in the Los Angeles Unified School District, the largest local authority in the state, approximately 80 different mother tongue, or home, languages are represented. With regards to language proficiency, the California State Department of Education reports that approximately 10 per cent of all students in special education are limited in their English proficiency (LEP).

Meeting tomorrow's needs

To meet the needs of these culturally and linguistically diverse pupils, one would hope that there would be a sufficient number of bilingual teachers; however, this is not the case. Over the next ten years, a shortage of 20,000 bilingual teachers is expected. Furthermore, statistics are not kept on the number of bilingual special education teachers at either the local or state level. Yet, according to officials at the state and local level, the need for bilingual special educators is great.

The projection for the future in terms of the cultural and language diversity of the school population is continued change. However, *current training for special educators is not prepared to meet this change*. Yates (1988) stated that there is great contrast between the demographic characteristics of the United States and the demography of the discipline of special education. For the most part, research, which is the foundation for teacher education, has been conducted by White, English-speaking professionals who have largely ignored important issues such as ethnicity, second language acquisition and non-biased assessment, which relate to the current school population.

Mother tongue instruction

Research has supported the need for LEP pupils with special education needs to be instructed in the language that is most comprehensible to them. Ortiz and Yates (1989) suggested that if these pupils do not master their native or primary language that they will have even greater difficulty developing skills in a second language and may also experience difficulty in developing cognitive skills. Ortiz and Yates also recognised that in cases where there is a lack of bilingual special educators such as in the cases where low-incidence languages are spoken by pupils such as Russian and Vietnamese, special educators must also become proficient in English as a Second Language (ESL) techniques.

The Loyola Marymount University (LMU) special education training program

Before 1985, the training program at LMU was very similar to the majority of training programs throughout the United States. The research which supported the training was based on studies which focused primarily on White middle-class pupils with specific, moderate and severe learning difficulties. The director and staff were White and monolingual English-speaking and had very little experience of working with culturally and linguistically diverse pupils.

However, it was soon recognised that the pupils with learning difficulties in the public school classes in California differed greatly from those commonly studied in research. The pupils were primarily Hispanic or African-American and spoke a mother tongue other than standard American English.

In addition, before 1985, the majority of the teachers who were being trained at the University were White and monolingual English speakers. Obviously, there was an incongruity between the training of these teachers and their cultural and linguistic compatibility with the needs of the pupils in the schools. To address this need, a decision was made to radically change the training.

Stages of development

The current program has gone through two distinct stages as evaluation data provided important information on the appropriateness of the goals of the program and the effectiveness of the program to reach its goals.

Stage 1   Since mother tongue instruction was considered to be a very important component of the education of LEP pupils with special education needs, the goal of the first stage was to train *bilingual* special educators by recruiting bilingual candidates and by requiring English-speaking monolingual candidates to become proficient in a second language (Spanish or an Asian language) while completing special education coursework where bilingual and multicultural competencies had been infused. However, the first step in the development of the program was to identify the competencies to be included in it. Since very few bilingual special education programs existed in the United States before 1985, it was decided to review the published literature and to conduct research in school districts which had bilingual special education programs in order to develop the most appropriate competencies for working with CLD pupils with specific, moderate and severe learning difficulties.

Over one hundred competencies were developed in the areas of assessment, instruction, curriculum, materials, program modification, counseling and school/community relations. However, to summarise these competencies, they are similar to the following general guidelines developed by Baca and Amato (1989, p. 169):

(1) The desire to work with the culturally and linguistically different exceptional child.
(2) The ability to work effectively with parents of these students.
(3) The ability to develop appropriate individual educational plans (IEPs) for these students.
(4) Knowledge and sensitivity toward the language and the culture of the group to be served.
(5) The ability to teach English as a second language to the students.
(6) The ability to conduct non-biased assessment with culturally and linguistically different exceptional students.
(7) The ability to use appropriate methods and materials when working with these students.

The specific competencies of the program were reviewed by a 'Blue Ribbon Panel' of bilingual special education experts from around the United States and were found to be appropriate for the program. These competencies were then infused into existing modules or classes. No new modules or classes were added to the program.

Evaluation of Stage 1   Stage 1 existed for three years and during that time the program underwent a formative and summative evaluation. In order to determine if the program was being implemented as initially planned, it was decided to evaluate the implementation of the program at the end of Year 1. Project staff and students were interviewed and student files were reviewed to determine how students were selected for the project as well as to determine the students' background characteristics. The Blue Ribbon Committee was also asked to evaluate the program's competencies in terms of their importance for training bilingual special educators.

Year 2 emphasised the monitoring of the program. The following questions were asked:

(1) What are the indications that the students are progressing satisfactorily?
(2) How are competencies assessed?
(3) What services/instruction does the project provide?

Again, interviews with the project staff provided the data.

Year 3 examined the effect of the project. It was important to determine the effects that had resulted from the project as well as how students perceived their abilities to have changed as a result of the project.

Conclusions from evaluation data for Stage.1 Apart from common implementation problems such as coordination and hiring of staff, the most serious problems came from a difficulty in recruiting teachers for the project as well as the initial development and infusion of the bilingual/multicultural competencies into the existing program. The pool of teachers in ordinary education who are bilingual is very small, thus making recruitment for special education even more difficult. Monolingual English-speaking teachers were hesitant to enroll since they assumed that they must be bilingual in order to be admitted to the program.

Infusion of bilingual/multicultural competencies into existing coursework was difficult since it took at least one year to identify the necessary competencies and have them evaluated by the Blue Ribbon Committee. Furthermore, university lecturers had to become familiar with the new coursework and found that there was insufficient time to teach both the old and new information.

Another important area of concern was the lack of appropriate bilingual special education training sites. Since this field is relatively new, there are few classrooms with bilingual special education teachers who can supervise trainees.

Positive results from the evaluation indicated that the majority of the students in the program 'felt that the program provided them with the necessary skills to teach in bilingual special education programs' (Solorzano, 1988a, p.7). In particular, some of the students 'felt they were more sensitive to culturally different students, while others noted that they learned new techniques in English as a Second Language (ESL) and Spanish language instruction' (Solorzano, 1988b, p.3).

The results of the evaluation of the Blue Ribbon Committee identified the most important competencies for the program. They included the following:

(1) The ability to *use observation, assessment instruments and procedures, as well as clinical teaching to develop individualised instruction* in academic, language, social-emotional/adaptive behavior, cognitive, motor, self-help and critical/functional skills of CLD pupils with specific, moderate and severe learning difficulties *in light of cultural and language factors*;

(2) the ability to *assess the learning style* of CLD pupils with specific, moderate and severe learning difficulties to facilitate instruction;

(3) the ability to *identify conditions necessary for establishing a positive relationship between school and home* for CLD pupils with specific, moderate, and severe learning difficulties *in light of cultural and language factors*;

(4)   the ability to *analyze and evaluate the use of various instructional approaches with both elementary and secondary* CLD pupils with specific, moderate, and severe learning difficulties *in light of cultural and language factors.*

The following competencies were identifed as the most important for special education resource or support specialists:

(1)   The ability to *work with parents of CLD pupils during the referral process in order to defuse anxiety and provide information for decision making*;
(2)   the ability to *explain selected assessment results to the assessment team, parents, and referred CLD pupils in a manner which is understandable to them*;
(3)   the ability to *plan and implement an inservice on the topic of utilising systematic observation for referral* of CLD pupils, incorporating the impact of cultural and linguistic characteristics and child-rearing practices;
(4)   the ability to *use appropriate observation techniques when evaluating situations which are of concern*;
(5)   the ability to *provide ordinary classroom teachers with information about CLD pupils which might reduce the number of inappropriate referrals*; and
(6)   the ability to *identify which agencies provide services appropriate for CLD pupils.*

Another concern of the evaluation was the contribution by the program to the pool of qualified bilingual special education teachers. The evaluation revealed some interesting data in terms of planning at the state level in California. As of 1988, the State of California had no specific figures on the need for bilingual special education teachers although it was generally recognized by officials who were interviewed that there was a need for these teachers. In fact, officials at the state level are frequently contacted by officials at the local authority level requesting training of bilingual special education teachers, especially Asian (Chinese, Vietnamese, Cambodian, etc.) speaking teachers. Therefore, the 18 bilingual special education teachers who graduated from the program are making an immediate contribution to the field, but 'determining the actual impact that the program has on the pool of bilingual special education teachers cannot easily be ascertained at this time' (Solorzano, 1988b, p.12).

   In addition to the information provided by the formal evaluation, important information was gathered by program staff. In particular, although monolingual English speaking teachers were required to develop proficiency in a second language, this requirement became a significant source of frustration and the students were making limited progress. Since the students were having difficulty becoming proficient in the second language within the time constraints of the program and the time commitment distracted the students from the courses, it was decided to eliminate this requirement. The program, however, was still committed to instruction in the mother tongue.

It was also concluded by the staff that many CLD pupils come from language backgrounds other than Spanish or Asian languages, i.e. Russian, Armenian, Farsi, Hebrew. Therefore, it would be important for special education teachers to be trained in the use of ESL techniques. Consequently, it was decided to continue the program with the following changes.

Stage 2

(1)   Teachers who were already bilingual would be the focus of the program as well as African-American teachers.
(2)   White monolingual English-speaking teachers would also be recruited but would be required to complete four modules which would lead to their authorization as ESL teachers.
(3)   Four modules leading to authorization in ESL, as approved by the State of California, would be added to the program. These modules were, 1. Second Language Acquisition, 2. Applied Linguistics, 3. ESL Methodology, and 4. Intercultural Communication.
(4)   The title of the program was changed from *bilingual* to *crosscultural* special education. This change in title communicated to prospective candidates that the program involved many languages and cultures and that candidates did not have to become bilingual. Even bilingual teachers would learn crosscultural strategies which would enable them to be effective teachers with pupils from many cultural backgrounds.

Evaluation of the first year of Stage 2   Given the changes in Stage 2, the major focus of the evaluation again was to determine if the students profited from the program in their present jobs. The majority of students felt that they had gained a great deal from the program in a variety of ways and that they had learned many assessment techniques, instructional strategies, and program designs targeted to CLD pupils that were very helpful in their current jobs. In particular, one teacher mentioned how she had moved Spanish-speaking students into English using the skills she had learned in the program by using the Sheltered English approach to teach content material. Another student developed a systems approach for assessment to measure English proficiency and readiness for ESL instruction (Perez, 1989).

The evaluation of the second year is currently under way and will investigate if the graduates are actually using the skills gained from the program in their jobs. To accomplish this, employers of the graduates will be contacted and will be asked to comment on the graduates' job performance.

Program replication

As school populations in countries around the world become more culturally and linguistically diverse, more teacher education programs will be attempting to prepare their students to meet this challenge. It may be helpful, therefore, to examine the experience of the program at Loyola Marymount University in order to assist in the replication of its efforts at other universities and institutes of higher education. First, the process of ongoing evaluation has been critical to the success of the LMU program. It was very important to identify the goals of the program and to monitor the implementation of the program to meet these goals, as well as to identify the effects of the program.

Second, the program revealed that although it is highly desirable for teachers to become bilingual or multilingual, in many cases it is not realistic. Teachers, instead, must learn to help their students become bilingual through collaborative efforts with speakers of the students' mother tongue while also assisting the students to develop proficiency in the second language. Teachers must also become aware of their own degree of sensitivity to other cultures as well as learning to develop teaching strategies which are culturally sensitive.

Conclusion

Based on the demographics of the United States, and California in particular, it is evident that there is a great shortage of teachers who can work effectively with CLD pupils. To address this need, Loyola Marymount University has developed a training program to prepare teachers to work with these pupils. An important component of this program has been its evaluation efforts which have led the program to be more responsive to both the needs of the students as well as to the field. Hopefully, the description of the development of this program will be of assistance to other training programs as they also attempt to better prepare special education needs teachers to meet the needs of multicultural society.

24

References

Baca, L. and Amato, C. (1989) 'Bilingual special education: training issues', *Exceptional Children*, **56**, 2, 168–73

California State Department of Education (1990) *Pupil Count*. Sacramento: Author.

California Tomorrow (1988) *Crossing the Schoolhouse Border*. San Francisco: Author.

Ortiz, A. A. and Yates, J. R. (1989) in Baca, L. and Cervantes, H. T. (Eds), *The Bilingual Special Education Interface* (pp. 183–203). Columbus: Merrill.

Perez, M. (1989) *'Loyola Marymount University bilingual special education personnel preparation program: second cycle first year evaluation'*. Unpublished report. Pasadena: Educational Testing Service.

Solorzano, R. W. (1988a) *'Loyola Marymount University bilingual special education personnel preparation program: second year evaluation'*. Unpublished report. Pasadena: Educational Testing Service.

Solorzano, R. W. (1988b) *'Loyola Marymount University bilingual special education personnel preparation program: third year evaluation'*. Unpublished report. Pasadena: Educational Testing Service.

Yates, J. R. (1988) 'Demography as it affects special education', in Ortiz, A. A. and Ramirez, B. A. (Eds), *Schools and the Culturally Diverse Exceptional Student: Promising Practices and Future Directions* (pp. 1–5). Reston: Council for Exceptional Children.

CHAPTER 3

System Supplied Information and the Identification of Staff Training Needs

Mel Myers and Roger Solomon

This chapter reports on the use of System Supplied Information (SSI), a methodology developed by a team of psychologists at Birmingham University (Myers *et al.*, 1989) to establish the particular training needs of staff dealing with problems related to the integration of children with special educational needs. Particular attention is paid to the way in which the materials and processes of SSI can be modified by the users to respond to the requirements and constraints of the host organisation and the broad political context in which the SSI project is being implemented.

General background

In the UK the 1981 Education Act gave statutory impetus to the integration of children with special educational needs in mainstream education and contained clear implications for the organisation and management of schools. In particular, it led to a recognition of the need to develop whole school approaches for children with learning difficulties. This type of approach would refer to the school's overall organisation, curriculum and methodology.

The Act also gave statutory effect to the recommendations of the Warnock Committee leading to a broader concept of special education based on the wide range of learning difficulties which children experience. The Report recommended that the planning of services for children should be based on the assumption that about one in six children at any time and up to one in five children at some time during their school career require some form of special educational provision. The majority of these children must be catered for in normal school settings.

It should be stressed that the concept of special educational need described above is not based on the notion that ordinary school policy and practice is necessarily appropriate for children with special educational needs without further adaptation and modification. Rather, what seems to be necessary is a planned response to ensure that the learning difficulties of children are recognised and taken into account and also that the responsibilities of all staff for these are given due emphasis and acknowledgement.

An allied consideration is the extent to which a child's special educational need should be seen as occurring within a given context, so that it is recognised and defined in terms of interaction with the learning environment. This of course includes the quality and degree of help received from home and school and must involve all aspects that relate to that child's schooling. It should be stressed that special educational need is an interactive concept and this places a requirement on professionals involved in education to recognise that the school itself is a potential creator of special educational needs. If this is acknowledged, the importance of developing effective whole school approaches becomes readily apparent as does the need to contain the necessary adaptations and modifications within a sensitive process for the management of change.

A crucial element in the change process related to the development of whole school approaches for children with special educational needs is the identification of relevant staff training needs. In this context, it is important that the needs of individual staff should be enmeshed with those of the organisation as a whole in order to ensure a coordinated programme of development. It is also important that the planning, implementation and evaluation of training should fit coherently into the school's overall development plan.

It will be obvious that the process referred to above cannot be considered in isolation and that it will take place in the social, demographic and legislative context of the area and country in which it occurs. Training staff to meet special educational needs will therefore reflect this and will need to accommodate different sets of demands such as those emanating from the discrepancies between American and British legislation. Nonetheless, the principles for identifying training needs and subsequently planning, implementing and evaluating training may enjoy a certain universality of application.

System Supplied Information (SSI) is an approach which enables school staff in any country (at least, those with a broadly democratic ideology) to identify staff training needs within the context of whole school approaches to special educational need and to manage the subsequent process of change with due sensitivity. The adaptability of SSI will be made apparent and explained more fully in the following section.

SSI – a flexible framework for whole-school development

SSI was developed to assist those in education who were trying to bring about appropriate and durable change in schools and colleges (whether they were within organisations or acting as external support services to organisations). It consists of a set of materials (presented as a set of five files) which can be used by staff to guide them through the stages of an SSI project: introduction to the concepts and materials, collecting information (from staff, students, governors, parents and/or local employers), summarising and making sense of the collected information, planning and costing appropriate action, and evaluating outcomes and processes.

The development of SSI was informed by two main considerations. First, that, as far as possible, change should relate to the perceived needs of the staff within the organisation. Second, that there needed to be an established framework within the organisation which was not imposed upon but which came from the personnel who make up the organisation and which would enable time and personnel to be allocated for the implementation, maintenance and on-going evaluation of change (i.e., so that the change process could be *built in* rather than *bolted on* to the organisation).

The concept of users being able to adapt the materials and processes is fundamental to SSI and is made possible in three main ways. In the first case, the direction and focus of an SSI project is steered by the subjective perceptions of staff (and pupils), thus ensuring sensitivity to local and current needs.

Second, understanding the principles which inform the processes and materials of SSI enables staff to modify the approach to suit specific local needs. Thus, the checklists supplied as part of the materials can be modified, or new ones generated on the basis of the principles of asking job-related or functional questions and of valuing subjective perceptions. Guidelines on how to do this are contained within the materials.

Third, staff are encouraged to adopt a process of progressive refinement in which the outcomes of any one stage of a project are used to decide the direction and focus of any further action. For instance, the outcomes of a survey of staff concerns to do with study skills might indicate that most staff felt that pupils about to embark on assessed externally examined courses had a major need and that some members of staff felt that they themselves would benefit from further training in this area. On the basis of this data, the members of the steering group coordinating the project might recommend that a more detailed survey be made of third-year pupils' needs and/or that suitable in-service training on study skills be made available for all or some members of staff. These initiatives would themselves be monitored and their outcomes used to decide the need for further planning and action until the original concerns to do with study skills had been satisfactorily addressed.

Background to the project

The project reported in this chapter took place in a comprehensive school in a Welsh Local Authority where the integration of children with special educational needs was very much on the agenda. The school was located in an area of considerable disadvantage, where the incidence of unemployment was significantly higher than the national average and the level of economic hardship one of the most acute in Wales. Without making assumptions of causality, it was apparent that, against this backcloth, the incidence of children with special educational needs in school was disproportionate and the results of standardised attainment tests had indicated that the figure was well in excess of Warnock's 20 per cent.

A problem confronting the Headteacher was the need to progress from a traditional remedial teaching situation within which children with the most acute special needs had been segregated, to one in which the children were largely integrated and in which the scope of the problem as defined by the broader concept of special needs was accepted by the staff. It was evident that this would involve a substantial degree of awareness raising for mainstream staff and that this should include a strong element of demystification with regard to the role of the teacher in special education. In short, the change process would need to be handled with care and sensitivity.

In this particular school, SSI was already in use and a previous project had been concerned with extending curricular access for less able pupils. In practical terms, this meant that a steering group was already in place and that its members had experience and understanding of the SSI process. The project had evolved with support from the local educational psychologist and consultancy from a univeristy-based senior educational psychologist who was one of the authors of SSI.

Support was also available at a higher level in the sense that the SSI project had not been allowed to develop in isolation but from the outset had been considered within the context of the local authority (LEA). Accordingly, a management group was set up at the outset to consider the role that SSI might play within the authority and to monitor its usage. One other comprehensive had been involved in the original project concerned with curricular access and that had been supported with additional funding. The management group was able to support and sanction a further allocation of funding to the second project described in this chapter.

The main purpose of the management group was to effect a reciprocal relationship between the LEA and those involved in the project at local level. It included a senior administrator, a senior staff development officer, the headteachers and steering group coordinators from the schools involved and the two educational psychologists mentioned previously. The group was to ensure that SSI initiatives would evolve within the framework of LEA policy and legislative requirements, would oversee the allocation of resources where possible and would receive feedback on outcomes and developments and project evaluation. The group would also provide a platform for the dissemination of good practice. In the event, funding was arranged for a training project involving a further six schools.

The project described in this chapter was therefore able to benefit from high-level support in the form referred to above and was given impetus by the provision of extra funding. Within the school, it was decided that the main focus would be the training needs of mainstream staff who were dealing with special needs children and would be required to assume responsibilities that they had not considered before. In addition to the resource benefit mentioned above, it was possible for the steering group to refer to the management group at various stages during the course of the project, thereby creating a dialogue that was of great value in sustaining their work.

An aspect of the project which deserves mention is that it provided an opportunity to enhance the role of the educational psychology service in its work with schools. System Supplied Information involves an attempt to apply psychology to real-life problems and to provide solutions at the level of organisation. The opportunity to work with the school at this level in more depth than had been attempted before was something of a breakthrough in the area of close collaboration between educational psychologists and teachers and provided a model of working that could be generalised to other situations. A valuable spin-off from the project was that it demonstrated that educational psychologists could contribute to the review of schools as organisations and in so doing work more closely with teachers in general than had been the case before.

The stages in which this particular project developed are described in the following section.

The project timeline and main events

A Steering Group (SG), chosen to be representative of staff opinion, experience and seniority, had been set up during the previous SSI project on curricular access. They were happy to coordinate the project which enabled the school to benefit from the learning which had already occurred.

The school had already had a two-day INSET programme on the theme of self-supported study, but the major concern of staff when their opinion was sought by the SG (Stage 3 above), was still to do with

Figure 3.1   Summary of events

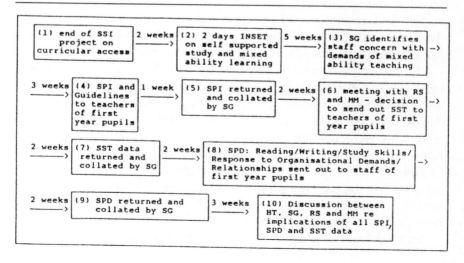

the demands which mixed ability teaching placed upon them (including the need to create additional teaching materials to meet a wide range of attainments and the need to adjust their teaching to accommodate different rates of progress within the class), particularly in the context of other pressures created, for example, by the need to implement the National Curriculum.

As a result of the information from Stage 3, the SG decided on a three-pronged investigation:

(a) to survey the needs of pupils in the first year, as perceived by staff;
(b) to obtain more detailed information on pupils identified in (a) as appropriate;
(c) to establish the range of concerns which staff involved with first-year pupils might have with regard to class contact and other aspects of their teaching role.

The SG intended to use the data from (a), (b) and (c) (together with the outcomes of the recent INSET, and in the context of the school's policy on mixed ability teaching) to help them to determine staff training needs.

The SG decided to use the SPI (Staff perception of Pupil needs – Initial) checklist for step (a). SPI lists eight areas of possible concern (reading, written work, maths, spoken communication, relationships in school, response to school's organisational demands, physical skills and study skills) and simply requires teachers to list, for each of their teaching groups, any pupil they perceive to have a problem with any of the eight areas in their subject in that teaching group.

For each of the eight areas of SPI a corresponding, and more detailed, functional checklist (SPD: Staff perception of Pupil needs – Detailed) was available. The SG agreed to use whichever of these checklists was indicated by the returns from the SPI checklists in step (a).

For step (c), the SG again decided to use one of the existing SSI functional checklists (SST: Staff perception of Staff needs – Teaching) which covered preparation for and follow-up of lessons, as well as concerns with class contact and teaching itself.

It was felt appropriate by the SG to carry out step (c) before step (b). This allowed plenty of time to collate the information from step (a) as a basis for deciding which of the eight SPD forms to use. Additionally, because it took more time to complete SPD than either of the other checklists (SPI requires roughly 5 minutes and SST roughly 10 minutes per teaching group, whilst each SPD checklist requires about 1 minute per pupil for each pupil identified in each teaching group), the SG felt that the time load on colleagues would be more equitable.

Together with the senior management team, the SG held an induction meeting, prior to stage 4 above, for all members of staff involved with first year pupils (effectively, the whole staff). During the meeting they outlined: the background to and purpose of the proposed project, the checklists to be used, the estimated timescale, the process for (and personnel involved with) the distribution and retrieval of checklists and associated guidelines and the way in which the information would be summarised, fed back to all colleagues and utilised in the further planning of staff training.

Results

1 SPI

The SPI checklists were summarised, using the SSI collation sheets, over all subjects and for all teaching groups in the first year. The results are shown in Figure 3.2 and indicate that reading, writing, study skills and response to school's organisational demands were all high scoring areas.

Because the information was collected by the school staff, the SG was able to make sense of the data in the context of their knowledge of the school in a way which would not have been possible for an outside agent; the SG noted, for instance, that a score of, say, 89 did not

Figure 3.2 Summary of SSI returns

	READING	WRITTEN WORK	MATHS	SPOKEN COMMUNICATION	RELATIONSHIPS IN SCHOOL	RESPONSE TO SCHOOL'S ORG. DEMANDS	PHYSICAL SKILLS	STUDY SKILLS
YEAR 1	89	87	27	55	44	67	36	89

Figure 3.3. Summary of SST returns

YEAR:

SUBJECT / DEPT:

TEACHER / TEACHING GROUP:	PREPARATION FOR & FOLLOW-UP OF TEACHING														
	PREPARING LESSONS			MARKING			RECORDING INDIVIDUAL CHILDREN'S PROGRESS			SPECIFYING LESSON AIMS			SPECIFYING LONGER TERM AIMS		
	Tl	R	Tr	Tl	R	Tr	Tl	R	Tr	Tl	R	Tr	Tl	R	Tr
1.															
2.															
3.															
4.															
5.															
6.															
7.															
8.															
9.															
10.															
11.															
12.															
Grand SUMMARY Tl/R/Tr. TOTAL	11	7	4	11	0	2	16	1	1	6	1	4	4	1	4
Grand SUMMARY TOTAL SCORE	32			27			39			11			12		

TEACHER / TEACHING GROUP:	TEACHING LESSONS																							
	LESSON LENGTH			NO. OF PERIODS TIMETABLED FOR TEACHING THIS GROUP			IMPLEMENTING LESSON AIMS			USING TEACHING AIDS & MATERIALS			CLASSROOM ORGANISATION			CLASSROOM MANAGEMENT			LESSON INTERRUPTIONS DUE TO YOUR OTHER DUTIES			LESSON INTERRUPTIONS DUE TO OTHER SCHOOL ACTIVITIES		
	Tl	R	Tr	Tl	R	Tr	Tl	R	Tr	Tl	R	Tr	Tl	R	Tr	Tl	R	Tr	Tl	R	Tr	Tl	R	Tr
1.																								
2.																								
3.																								
4.																								
5.																								
6.																								
7.																								
8.																								
9.																								
10.																								
11.																								
12.																								
Grand SUMMARY Tl/R/Tr. TOTAL	9	0	2	5	0	1	5	2	4	3	8	4	4	6	4	3	7	5	4	0	0	3	0	0
Grand SUMMARY TOTAL SCORE	27			22			23			27			29			22			15			16		

necessarily mean that 89 different pupils were perceived to have reading problems but, rather, that the total was made up of a number of different pupils together with a group of pupils who were perceived to have a problem by a number of teachers (that is, one or more pupils might be represented a number of times by different teachers).

The SG also noted that a particular group of pupils might account for some of the perceived problems in each of the eight areas, and with the help of a member of the IT department who was on the SG they were able to carry out computer analyses which showed both these assumptions to be correct; that is that there was a group of pupils who accounted for a large proportion of the scores within an area and across the eight different areas. In particular, the analysis revealed a large overlap between perceived curricular and behaviour problems.

2 SST

The SST returns were summarised using SSI collation sheets, and a copy of the results is shown in Figure 3.3. The three main areas of concern among the staff who taught the first year pupils were; Recording Individual Children's Progress, Preparing Lessons and Classroom Organisation. (Marking, Lesson Length and Using Teaching Aids & Materials were next in perceived priority).

For each of the main areas of the checklist, staff were also able to indicate whether, if they had a concern within any area, there was also a concern to do with Time (Ti), Resources (R) and/or Training (Tr). As can be seen from Figure 3.3., whilst there is some concern regarding Resources and Training for a number of areas, the concern about Time runs across all 13 areas.

3 SPD

For reasons to do with economy of space, the information from the five SPD checklists has been summarised (see Table 3.1) rather than presented as a copy of the original SPD Collation forms.

It will help in understanding the results in Table 3.1 to recall that SPDs were only distributed to the staff concerned with teaching groups which included pupils identified from the SPI; and to know that for each pupil, on each of the five SPD checklists, the teacher gave a rating on a 5-point scale:

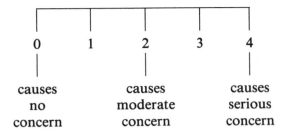

and when each checklist was summarised over all teachers and all teaching groups, the high scores only (3 and 4) were totalled and expressed as a percentage of all the pupils in the teaching groups concerned for that checklist.

Outcomes

The SG met with the headteacher and the two authors (stage 10) in order to prepare outline plans for staff training. In doing so, they took into account both the context (the school's mixed ability teaching policy and the developments which had arisen from the self-supported study INSET course) and the results from the various SSI surveys summarised in the previous section.

The relatively large number of pupils shown by the SPI and SPD surveys to have special educational needs made recourse to a withdrawal system inappropriate, and it was helpful to the SG discussions that the data from the staff themselves reinforced the need for a mixed ability teaching policy.

Within this mixed ability teaching context, the SG felt that they needed to put forward a plan for staff training which would overcome the reading and study skills problems by enabling the pupils to work from their own level within a particular subject, and in such a way that staff could make available a wide range of work without this impinging on their already minimal available time.

In general terms the SG saw two aspects to this plan. First, the training needed to be such that it would enable staff to encourage independent learning skills by the pupils – so that they would become proactive rather than passive with regard to their own learning processes and so become more involved and motivated (thereby reducing problems to do with study skills, bringing the right materials and handing work in on time). Second, the training needed to encourage and enable staff themselves to move from a didactic role to

Table 3.1

READING	% high scores
Reading accurately	28
Understanding written material	25
Reading with reasonable speed	28
Locating and extracting information	22
Reading aloud ½uently	13

WRITTEN WORK

Scores for legibility, accuracy, etc. ranged from 6–9 and were not considered to be as significant as from other areas.

RELATIONSHIPS	% high scores
Other pupils in class	22
Other pupils out of class	10
You as teacher in class	17
You as teacher out of class	2
Adults other than teachers in class	0.4
Adults other than teachers out of class	0.4

RESPONSE TO SCHOOL'S ORGANIZATIONAL DEMANDS	% high scores
Attendance at school	2
Attendance at lessons	7
Punctuality for school	-
Punctuality for lessons	3
Following rules and routines	18
Finding way around school	2
Bringing appropriate equipment and materials to school	18
Giving homework in on time	13

STUDY SKILLS	% high scores
Concentrating on task	30
Completing set work when supervised	32
Completing set work when not supervised	34
Selecting and completing own tasks	33
Organising own timetable	33
Locating and extracting information relevant to task	34
Summarising and representing data	27

one where they were facilitating the (increasingly independent) learning skills and processes of the pupils.

Pressure on teacher time, it was felt, should be reduced in two ways: with pupils increasingly agreeing a 'learning contract' with the teacher, they should be able to proceed at the most appropriate rate and to use the most appropriate materials for each individual, thus saving the teachers from having to spend most of their time devising large amounts of work sheets or other teaching materials at all stages of the curriculum. In addition, with the teacher as facilitator rather than performing a 'chalk and talk' role, there should be fewer problems to do with lesson interruptions as these would affect the teacher but should not be disastrous for the pupils who would be able to continue, independently, with their contracts. The contracts, too, would furnish a basis for joint recording of the progress of individual pupils.

The outcome of the meeting was that the SG would formally propose to staff that there should be further INSET, the nature of which would encourage the pupils to be more independent in their learning and which would, at the same time, enable the staff to move further along the continuum from the classical teaching role towards being facilitators of learning.

Conclusion

This chapter has reported on the way in which a typical secondary comprehensive school has used SSI both to establish the training needs of its staff with regard to the special educational needs of first-year pupils and, at the same time, to develop a framework within the school, through the Steering Group, which enabled it to respond systematically to those needs and in a way which gave ownership of the process (and, hence, commitment to the outcomes) to the staff as a whole.

The SSI project was also a positive example of collaborative working both from the point of view of the high level support and monitoring from the LEA management group, and also with regard to the involvement of the School Psychological Service (SPS). Because SSI kept ownership of the problem, the information and the planning within the school, the SPS was able to make skills and expertise available in such a way that they came on line as and when the school needed them.

38

References

Myers, M., Cherry, C., Timmins, P., Brzezinska, H., Miller, P. and Willey, R. (1989) 'System Supplied Information (SSI): How to assess needs and plan effectively within schools/colleges', *Educational Psychology in Practice*, **4**, 91–6.

CHAPTER 4

Specialist Settings: An Under-used Resource for Teacher Training

Keith Bovair

The education of pupils with special educational needs in ordinary schools is growing internationally. In the United States, the mainstreaming movement of the 1970s is being re-evaluated and is re-emerging as the 'Regular Education Initiative' (Stainback, Stainback and Forest, 1989). In Canada, in the Province of Ontario, two separate school boards have adopted the stance of 'Total Inclusion' of all pupils, with a wide cross-section of special needs, in ordinary settings (Bovair, 1990, Flynn and Kowalczyk, 1989). Also, it can be seen in Great Britain that, 'Developments overall have been cautiously integrationist, as advocated in the Warnock Report, but not necessarily planned or monitored with the kind of rigour the report advocated' (Sect.73, Special Needs Issues, HMSO, 1990).

Still, with ever increasing numbers of children identified as having special educational needs being educated in ordinary schools, the question of appropriate teacher training must be considered. In the United States, *A Report Card on Special Education* (Harris *et al.*, 1989) noted that,

> while regular education teachers have an average of 3 to 4 students with disabilities in class for a portion of the day, a full 40% reported having no training in special education. Although two thirds of regular classroom teachers had attended in-service sessions designed to help

teach children with handicaps, this same number reported needing more 'background in special education...in order to make appropriate decisions about handicapped children'.

It has been attempted in Great Britain to permeate special educational needs issues into initial teacher training since the mid-1980s, but as identified by Her Majesty's Inspectors, it is 'By no means fully effective in existing courses generally...' (Special Needs Issues, HMSO, 1990). This does not mean that educators have not pursued courses and in-service training that would give them the depth of training they felt they needed. Often these experiences have dealt with theory or issues and when this has occurred, we have seen emerging the 'affective' teacher; one who has great empathy towards the right of access for students with special educational needs to a broad, balanced and differentiated curriculum and acceptance in the ordinary school setting. What is required for the 1990s is the 'effective' teacher; one who is capable of taking theory and turning it into good practice which will ensure the right of access to a broad, balanced and differentiated curriculum and acceptance in the ordinary school setting.

The following is intended to highlight the current feelings of teachers who have recently completed their initial teacher training, towards their specific training in the area of special educational needs and to highlight the role that specialist settings and special schools have to play in the 'effective' training of teachers.

Background

In Chapter 12 (Teacher Education and Training) of the Warnock Report, (DES, 1978) it was recommended that within the initial training of all teachers there should be an element on special educational needs. It suggested that options should be offered, allowing for students who so desired, to pursue this area in more depth. With a view to integrating children with special educational needs into the mainstream this was seen as the way ahead.

In June 1984, the Advisory Committee on the Supply and Education of Teachers submitted advice to the Secretary of State for Education and Science and the Secretary of State for Wales, in a report titled *Teacher Training and Special Educational Needs*. It took on the recommendation in the Warnock report that all initial teacher training courses should include certain elements concerned with special educational needs and recommended that those in post who have responsibility for children with special educational needs should have 'post experience' training. It recommended that initial teacher training courses which are intended to prepare students to work in specific types of special schools or in 'remedial departments', should be phased out. The staffing expertise on these courses would then be used to contribute to post experience and to the 'awareness' elements of general initial training courses (the 'permeation principle').

In the Department of Education and Science Circular 3/84, *Initial Teacher Training: Approval of Courses*, it states that students should:

> be prepared through their subject method work and educational studies to teach the full range of pupils whom they are likely to encounter in the ordinary school . . . should learn to recognise children who are very able or gifted and appreciate how their potential can be developed . . .
> be introduced to ways of identifying children with special educational needs, helped to appreciate what the ordinary school can and cannot do for such children and give some knowledge of the specialist help available and how it can be enlisted.

Yet, in a survey of 254 primary school teachers by Gipps, Gross and Goldstein (1987):

> Only 31 per cent of the teachers had had, or could remember having, any courses on teaching children with special needs in their initial training. Happily, the situation with regard to in-service training was rather better: overall, 47 per cent of the teachers had been on courses in the last five years and this varied by LEA (rather than age, experience or other qualifications) . . . However, 21 per cent of the teachers had had neither in-service training on special needs, nor any course on special needs or remedial teaching during their initial training.

Similar feelings towards the inadequacy of initial teacher training in the area of special educational needs were identified earlier by Nisbet, Shanks and Darling (1977) in 'A survey of teachers' opinions on the primary diploma course in Scotland', where '58% felt inadequately prepared for teaching slow learners and 6% said the topic had not been dealt with; 28% felt inadequately prepared for teaching handicapped children and 61% said the topic had not been dealt with'.

In 'The New Teacher in School', a survey by HM Inspectors in England and Wales (DES, 1987), it was identified that, 'disturbing proportions of all the new teachers in the 1987 survey emerged from training feeling less than adequately prepared for important areas such as teaching the less able and children with special educational needs' (Sect 1.38), and

Although the changes in Circular 3/84 should, in time, bring improvements in many of these areas, the survey raises the question of the depth to which they were dealt with in the courses followed by these new teachers. The brevity of the PGCE (Postgraduate Certificate in Education; a one year training course for graduates) raises the issue acutely. More attention needs to be given to defining the levels of competence in different professional skills which may reasonably be expected of teachers at the conclusion of their training. These levels of competence need to be understood and accepted by those responsible both for training and induction (Sect 1.41).

Research

As an educator in special education, I have been concerned about the preparation of students on initial teacher training courses to meet the needs of the growing population of children with special educational needs in ordinary schools. Also, I felt strongly that a proportion of children who were exhibiting learning difficulties were being referred for alternative specialist placements due to lack of strategies and support in those schools rather than lack of abilities on the part of the referring teachers. I wanted to look at teachers' starting points in training in the area of special educational needs.

In January 1989, I was offered a two-term secondment to research initial teaching training and special education needs issues, to enquire into the appropriateness of such training, and to identify future provision and content for such training. Also, I personally wanted to establish the use of specialist settings and special schools as training placements for students on initial teacher training.

In order to investigate the issues with which I was concerned I took advantage of induction courses being held in the winter of 1989, to survey primary trained teachers who were just entering the teaching profession (probationers) (Appendix 4.1). At that time there were 114 probationers in the county where I based my work and I received 84 replies to my survey. In these replies 38 colleges and universities were represented.

In reviewing literature from these institutions, their desires and/or requirements in the area of special educational needs and initial teacher training can be summarised as being that: first, students would come to identify and understand the more common learning difficulties; second, that all students would be presented with special educational needs issues; third, that lectures and discussions would be linked with practical teaching and assessments, and fourth, that options would be offered to develop further skills in the area of special educational needs.

Within these institutions the 'permeation principle' (that of injection of special needs issues into main subject areas), was developing. The 'permeation principle' was encouraged earlier by the Warnock Report, which 'included recommendations that a special education element for all students should be included in all courses of initial teacher training, and that wherever possible these courses should also offer options, thus enabling some to pursue their interest in their field in more depth' (Sect. 22, Special Needs Issues, HMSO, 1990).

Drawing out information from the survey (Appendix 4.1), four questions (1,5,7 and 9b) highlighted the students' exposure to specific areas of special needs in terms of specific training, types of children encountered while on teaching practice and visits to educational establishments and the special educational needs encountered during a teacher's first year (probationary year) of teaching. These are identified in Figure 4.1.

The types of exposure to children with special educational needs varied, as identified by question two (proportion of training devoted to special educational needs); it ranged from single lecture, single lecture and a visit, lectures and visits, a half-term course and a full-term course on the issues of special educational needs. Rather than permeation, there appears to be permutation.

In extracting information as to where students encountered children with special educational needs during their training, question four (contact with children with special educational needs outside teaching practice) and question six (contact with children with special educational needs while on teaching practice), identify that the majority of contacts with children with special educational needs took place in ordinary school settings. Question eight, which was concerned with where teaching practice took place, shows that initial teacher training rarely took place in specialist settings (only 2.38 per cent of those surveyed had teaching practice in specialist settings [class within ordinary school]; 2.38 per cent had teaching practice in a special unit [attached to an ordinary school] and 3.57 per cent had teaching practice within a special school).

Of the 84 probationers surveyed, 90.4 per cent of students had never been placed in a specialist setting for their initial teacher training. In other words specialist settings, where trained, skilled educators who have responsibility for children with special educational needs day to

Figure 4.1 Special educational needs encountered during a probationary year

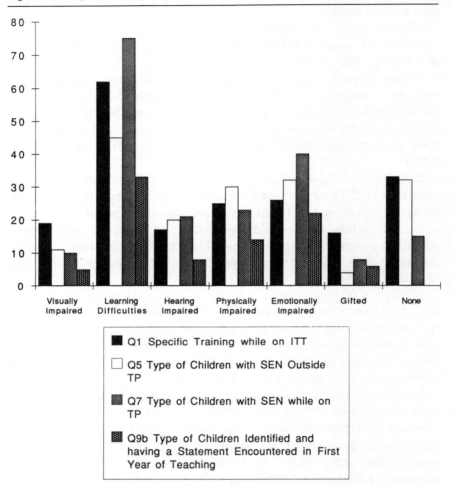

day, are not being drawn upon to increase the skills base of students in initial teacher training so that they may meet the needs of the growing population of children with special educational needs in the ordinary school.

The students appeared to express their feelings of lack of expertise by their replies to question ten: 93 per cent felt they were inadequately trained to meet children's special educational needs. Yet, these students were open to extended training. Question eleven (b) revealed that 52 per cent would accept opportunities for team teaching with a special needs teacher in their own classroom, 50 per cent showed a desire for team teaching experience with a special needs teacher in a specialist setting. Other areas which were identified as being relevant to the development of these teachers' skills were lectures in the area of special needs (19 per cent requested these), visits and observations of specialist settings (39 per cent) or a series of visits to a special school or unit (32 per cent).

What is clearly identified is that there is more to be done in initial teacher training. In the reply to question twelve, which asked for the teachers' final comments on the special educational needs element of training while on initial teacher training, 34 per cent felt their training was inadequate, 22 per cent felt more could be done to extend their adequacy in the area of special educational needs, 33 per cent made no comment and 11 per cent felt that the element of special educational needs while on initial teacher training was adequate.

Conclusions

> Teachers require better initial training, better induction in the schools where they take up their first post, better opportunities to acquire new classroom and managerial skills in the light of the changing demand and ever increasing speed of change and innovation (Booth *et al.*, 1989).

The information collected bears this out.

Probationary teachers desire a greater depth of experience of special educational needs to meet their current perceived needs. A large proportion of them were not fully satisfied with their training in special educational needs while on initial teacher training, and yet a large proportion of students on initial teacher training were exposed to children with special educational needs. Probationary teachers are open to working collaboratively with other colleagues to extend their knowledge and their ability to meet the needs of children with special educational needs. It is clear that specialist settings are under-used as placements for students on initial teacher training.

Initial teacher training for the past ten years has been gradually introducing an element of special educational needs into its courses. With the increase in numbers of children with special educational needs being maintained or placed in the mainstream, the greater the training need and the assurance of 'permeation' of special educational needs elements into all subject areas.

In the field of special education headteachers of special schools and heads of units and specialist settings have seen some growth of interest in the field of special needs amongst students in initial teacher training.

They may have hosted school visits which 'contributed' to the special needs element of initial teacher training. A few years ago, these visits were superficial, but with dialogue with training institutions, they have been attempting to create opportunities that will allow the students to study this area of education in more depth. One of these opportunities is described by Morag Styles and Catherine Pearce (1989) who decided to use a special school as one of the settings for their students' practical experience of teaching and observing children with special educational needs.

> In the summer of 1986 the English Department at Homerton College, Cambridge, decided to mount a course on Language and Special Needs in the Primary Curriculum which would be offered as an option to Year III students, and contribute to the first part of the Education Tripos. In the English curriculum courses in Years I and II, attention is paid to ways of helping those with problems in reading and writing, but we intended this course to focus on the wider issues of special needs, to give students the opportunity to respond to the needs of those children whom they were meeting on teaching practice and on leaving college.
>
> We planned that this course should from the beginning involve cooperation with local schools and teachers. We decided to devote half of the course to lectures followed by seminar discussions. The second half should involve practical work in school, helping a child with language and learning problems.
>
> The assignment was to be a 3,000 word case study of a child's strengths and weaknesses. The students were urged to focus on small areas of learning difficulty, in the hope that this might ensure success.

The student teachers' comments identify a very positive experience which hopefully will enhance their abilities as teachers.

> I think that if possible every student should have the opportunity to work with children with special needs and to understand how this kind of teaching compares with that of mainstream education. Most of all we should learn how to 'slow the system down and make the pupils shine'.
>
> The common platitude 'Begin with the child' had taken on renewed meaning. Merely presenting the same material at a lower level no longer seemed a viable manner of working, but by taking the lead from the child, his motivation and needs, I had found that more personally relevant and potentially successful learning could take place;

and last

> I have learned a great deal about the very nature of communication and

the ways in which a teacher can promote an environment in which a child feels confident enough to learn to verbalise effectively.

Traditionally, perhaps, primary school teachers have been receptive towards moves to encourage them to consider children with special educational needs. Maybe this is because they know that they will need strategies in coping with the needs of children who present learning difficulties until these needs are examined, assessed, re-examined, debated and finally met in a specialist setting or by receiving specialist support.

It is hoped, however, that the students quoted above have learned from these experiences, lessons which they will use in their teaching of all children and not just those identified as having special educational needs. For all children deserve this approach although the lesson is perhaps much more forcefully learned in a special setting. Yet 90 per cent of those surveyed had had no experience of initial teacher training in a specialist setting, forgoing the opportunity of acquiring skills at first hand which they would be able to use with all children in their classes and in all subject areas.

In the past, secondary school teachers concentrated in their training on expanding their subject specialism. Special schools were seen as a world apart and if children with special educational needs were thought of at all by the average teacher in training, it was generally assumed that the depth of knowledge they required could easily be provided by a special needs teacher – a non-specialist.

In the changing situation of today's classroom, not only are teachers much more likely to come across children with special educational needs but (let us hope) the prevailing attitude is that the subject specialist is in a good position to be able to take his or her subject and break down large areas of learning and knowledge into manageable units for children whose exploration of the subject may move at a slower pace. Indeed, a special school or unit may be the best place to see this in action and learn how to go about it oneself.

Over the past four years, the author has personally hosted students who were on the one year post-graduate certificate in education (PGCE) course in the Department of Education at the University of Cambridge. They had chosen the final three-week option offered to them, to work in a specialist setting. The experience was set up so that they had the opportunity to introduce their subject interest to pupils and they experienced how to make it accessible to a population of children with special educational needs.

Ten students a year came to the special school and were each assigned to a class in the senior part of the school. The numbers involved meant that on occasions there would be more than one student to each class group. The students had the opportunity to team teach with the class teacher in the area of their subject specialism and also to plan and teach lessons on their own to the class. They developed strategies for managing the behaviour problems the children presented and for overcoming other problems such as reluctance to learn, short attention span, poor concentration and writing difficulties.

There were benefits here for the class teacher too. Our students on the PGCE were well motivated and of a high calibre. Their presence meant that teachers were released to work on a one-to-one basis with individual children either within the group or alone in another room. These opportunities, which rarely present themselves, were gratefully received. The questions put by the students also meant that the teachers needed to be clear in their own mind about the reasons for their methods of teaching and gave them a chance to re-evaluate their stance, and very often to reassert the value of their own work.

It has been reported in interviews with the students over this period that they found this to be an invaluable part of their training in understanding the complexities of children with special educational needs and the means by which one as an educator can tackle the complexity of problems an individual child may present.

Several projects were undertaken by the students. One such project involved five senior pupils under the guidance of one of the students. Together they redesigned their classroom to convert a space into a quiet area for personal study. They designed the area, costed the project and presented their proposal to the senior management of the school. Upon acceptance they bought materials and decorated it for the pupils' use. Subject specialities in art, printmaking, science, geography, history and physical education also enriched the curriculum.

In dialogue with the students' supervisors, some of whom visited the school, it is clear that they also have been presented with an opportunity for a reappraisal of their own attitudes towards special schools. The special school could be seen as a relevant educational setting suitable for the practising of one's subject specialism and also for learning methods of managing behaviour problems and other lessons student teachers are keen to master.

To conclude, we need to be more daring in our approach to initial teacher training and special needs. We need centres where training and practice exist side by side, where a concentration on children with special educational needs is heightened, where all students, no matter where their area of educational interest lies, can be given the opportunity to present their subject to pupils who often need their learning experiences individualised and structured for them.

References

Advisory Committee on the Supply and Education of Teachers (1984) *Teacher Training and Special Educational Needs,* June, London: ACSET.

Booth, M., Furlong, J., Hargreaves, D.H., Reiss, M.J. and Ruthven, K. (1989) 'Teacher Supply and Teacher Quality, Solving the Coming Crisis', *Cambridge Education Papers No. 1*, Department of Education, University of Cambridge.

Bovair, K. (1990) 'A Visit to Canada and the USA: Special Educational Needs Provision'. Unpublished paper, Central Bureau, London.

Department of Education and Science (1978) *Special Educational Needs* (The Warnock Report). London: HMSO.

Department of Education and Science (1984) *Initial Teacher Training, Approval of Courses* (3/84). London: HMSO.

Department of Education and Science (1990) *Special Educational Needs in Initial Training* (18/90). London: HMSO.

Department of Education and Science (1987) *The New Teacher in School, A Survey by HM Inspectors in England and Wales*. London: HMSO.

Flynn, J. and Kowalczyk-McPhee, B. (1989) 'A School System in Transition', in Stainback, S., Stainback, W. and Forest, W. (Eds) *Educating All Students in the Mainstream of Regular Education*. Maryland: Paul H. Brooker Publishing.

Gipps, C., Gross, H. and Goldstein, H. (1987) *Warnock's Eighteen Percent, Children with Special Educational Needs in the Primary School*. London: Falmer Press.

Harris, L. *et al* (1989) 'International Centre for the Disabled Survey III: A Report Card on Special Education, New York', in Floviar, L. and West, J. *Beyond Access: Special Education in America*. Paper presented at the International Special Education Congress, University of Wales, Cardiff.

Nisbett, J., Shanks, D. and Darling, J. (1977) 'A survey of teachers' opinions on the primary diploma course in Scotland', *Scottish Educational Studies*, **9**, 2.

Stainback, S., Stainback, W. and Forest, M. (1989) *Educating All Students in the Mainstream of Regular Education*. Maryland: Paul H. Brooker Publishing.

Styles, M. and Pearce, C. (1989) 'Special Schools: A Setting for Initial Teacher Training', in Baker, D. and Bovair, K. (Eds) *Making the Special Schools Ordinary*, Vol. 1. London: Falmer Press.

Appendix 4.1

THE SURVEY

1. The areas which teachers identified as receiving specific training in special needs while on ITT:

	%
Visually Impaired	19
Learning Difficulties	62
Hearing Impaired	17
Physicall Impaired	25
Emotionally Impaired	26
Gifted	16
None	33

2. The proportion of training devoted to teaching children with special needs:

The range of reply was almost as varied as the number of students surveyed, ranging from single lecture to half-term to term to full year course on special needs.

3. Whether the training was sufficient in the area of SEN to meet their needs:

a. On Teaching Practice

	%
Yes	55
No	45

a. In their first year of teaching

	%
Yes	31
No	67
Blank	2

4. Contact with children with SEN during training outside of teaching practice:

	%
Observed child/ren in ordinary setting	39
Interacted with child/ren in ordinary setting	42
Observed child/ren with SEN in special unit	26
Interacted with child/ren with SEN in special unit	19
Observed child/ren with SEN in a special school	33
Interacted with child/ren with SEN in a special school	23
None	19

5. Type of children with SEN encountered outside of TP:

	%
Visually impaired	11
Learning Difficulties	45
Hearing Impaired	20
Physically Impaired	30
Emotionally Impaired	32
Gifted	4
None	32

Added to questionnaire

Severe learning	1
Blank	2

6. Contact with children with SEN while on TP.

	%
None	20
Observed child/ren in ordinary setting	24
Interacted with child/ren in ordinary setting	68
Observed child/ren with SEN in special unit	7
Interacted with child/ren with SEN in special unit	5
Observed child/ren with SEN in a special school	1
Interacted with child/ren with SEN in a special school	0

7. Contact while on TP with children who were:

	%
Visually Impaired	10
Learning Difficulties	75

Hearing Impaired	21
Physically Impaired	23
Emotionally Impaired	40
Gifted	8
None	15

Additional to survey

Specific Impairment	1
English as Second Language	1

8. TP that took place in:

	%
A Special Class	2.28
A Special Unit	2.38
A Special School	3.57
None	90.47

Additional to survey

Social Priority School	1.19

9.a. During first year in teaching, those having a child who had a Statement of Special Needs in their classroom.

	%
Yes	42
No	48
Don't Know	2

9.b. Those that had statemented children in their class during their first year in teaching identified their needs as:

	%
Visually Impaired	5
Learning Difficulties	33
Hearing Impaired	8
Physically Impaired	14
Emotionally Impaired	22
Gifted	6

Additional to survey

Special Needs Register	1
In Process	5
No Response	2

10. Did the teachers feel that the Special Needs element in their ITT was sufficient to cover their needs in their future career in teaching?

	%
Yes	5

No	93
Don't Know	1
Not enough practical	1

11.a. Did the teachers feel that their Education Authority should offer further training in Special Needs to probationary teachers as part of their first year of teaching?

	%
Yes	96
No	4

11.b. Teachers were then asked: If yes, what would you perceive as being most useful?

Series of lectures	19
Observation visits to special units and schools	39
Series of visits to one special unit or school	32
Team teaching with a special needs teacher in your classroom	52
Team teaching with a special needs teacher in their setting	50
Other (Visits to local Special Needs Centres, opportunity to work one to one with child with SEN, working on school policy)	5
No reply	2

12. In the final comments on the SEN element in ITT:

	%
No Comment	33
Inadequate	34
Okay	11
Various	8
Need extended support	14

CHAPTER 5

IT-INSET and Special Education

Alan Peacock and Christina Tilstone

Introduction

IT-INSET, which stands for Initial Training and In-Service Education of Teachers, is a unique method of improving practice in the classroom. As the basic principle of IT-INSET is the firm link between the initial training of students and the in-service education of practising teachers, it is school-based and school-focused.

Cruickshank (Ashton *et al.*, 1989, p. 3) in considering the nature of in-service education and IT-INSET, states that it is:

> about really meeting the needs of children through meeting the needs of staff.... (It should be) focused on what is happening in classrooms, what pupils are doing, and what teachers are trying to do with them.

In accepting this principle, the present authors emphasise that it applies equally to the initial training of teachers, and that a combination of INSET and IT will improve the quality of the practical curriculum. The strategies which IT-INSET embodies use the full potential of a team consisting of three groups of practioners: practising teachers; tutors involved in initial teacher training; and their students. Each team concentrates on an area of focus within the curriculum which has been identified by the class teacher as in need of development. This essentially practical approach, with its emphasis on the 'here and now' enhances the skills of all involved. For the teachers, IT-INSET is an exciting method of evaluating their current practice in the real world of the classroom; for the tutors it provides an invaluable and essential opportunity to refresh and reconsider classroom practice and meets some of the United Kingdom criteria for the 'recent, relevant and regular classroom experience' they are required to have by the Department of Education and Science Circular 24/89 (DES, 1989); and it offers the students, as 'learner-teachers', full involvement in practical teaching, curriculum development and comprehensive evaluation.

An IT-INSET team normally consists of a class teacher, a tutor and five or six students. However, in special needs work in special schools fewer students (3–4 per class) are involved. IT-INSET has been successfully adopted by 22 Institutions of Higher Education in the United Kingdom offering teacher-training courses, as part of their programmes for Bachelor of Education Degrees and Post Graduate Certificates in Education and normally run for at least one half-day per week during one term. It is currently being introduced into some teacher training institutions in Australia (Marks and Peacock, 1988).

Although it is usual for the topic or focus to be chosen by the class teacher alone, a team's way of working requires a collaborative decision. Each team is unique and will develop a distinctive approach, but a common framework is always adopted, namely:

- At least one hour per week is spent in the classroom teaching, recording and monitoring children's learning.
- Adequate time is allowed, outside the classroom, for the analysis and evaluation of the work in progress.
- All the participants are involved in all aspects of planning, teaching, observing and evaluating.

It is clearly essential, therefore, that the roles within the classroom, of observer, of record-keeper and of teacher are shared equally between all team members. Participation in the process outside the classroom allows the evidence gathered to be fully analysed and discussed, and ensures that the changes that are or are not made are based on the team's considered decisions. As the team is committed to improving the quality of children's learning, these discussions are structured to allow a detailed analysis and evaluation of the work, and lead into the planning of the next session. The roles of chairperson and note-taker may rotate. In the United Kingdom this approach lends itself to the use of the questions in the 'Curriculum in Action' pack from the Open University which many teams have found to be a helpful framework for evaluation:

What did the pupils actually do?
What were they learning?

How worthwhile was it?
What did I do?
What did I learn?
What do I intend to do now?
(Ashton *et al.*, 1980).

The goals of IT-INSET

The principles of IT-INSET described above take their direction from the concept of teaching as practical theorising. Theorising goes on all the time in classrooms, sometimes explicitly, but more often unnoticed. If we can make our theories explicit, by talking them through with colleagues, and if we can focus our theorising and observation on a specific dimension of children's learning, even the most habitual, taken-for-granted bases for action can be subject to modification.

This idea of the teacher as a practical theoriser is illustrated in Figure

Figure 5.1 The observation-theorising-teaching cycle

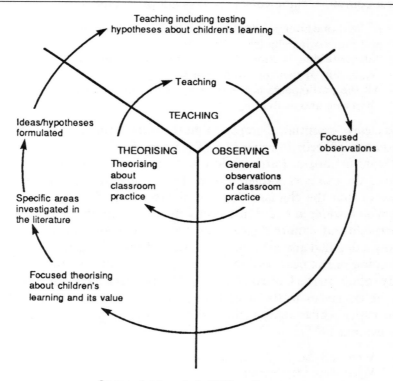

Source: Ashton *et al.*, 1989, p. 6.

5.1. The inner cycle represents what teachers normally do, namely make unsystematic observations whilst teaching, and use these to generate (implicit) theories which guide their subsequent teaching. For example, a teacher will often notice that some children finish a task more quickly than others, and will 'theorise' from this that they have finished quickly because . . . the children are the 'brightest', or the most interested, or the ones who work superficially, or whatever. As a consequence, he or she will deal with the situation by giving them extension material, by asking them to do it in more detail, or by using some other strategy.

The IT-INSET approach is illustrated by the outer cycle. Here, the team organises itself in a manner that enables an individual to undertake focused observations of children who finish quickly, in order that the subsequent discussion can concentrate on theorising about their learning. This will lead to the generation of several ideas for hypotheses within the team, which can then plan to test these ideas out during subsequent teaching, by further observation. For example, a number of ways of following up 'early finishers' might be tried, to see which is most appropriate, and more observational evidence will be fed back to the team.

The important characteristics of this practical theorising cycle are that:

(1) all members of the team are learning, and all share a responsibility for developing each other's understanding;
(2) looking at children's learning places the team's focus on evaluative competence, rather than on instructional competence;
(3) the cycle requires the development of teamwork and collaboration skills;
(4) outcomes relate directly to the curriculum as experienced by the children, and are therefore of immediate relevance to the teacher.

The approach can easily extend beyond the team to other teachers in a school, and has been used for whole-school curriculum evaluation as in the example described by Sewell (1987). When IT-INSET is working in this way to the benefit of all participants, it has been shown to be extremely cost effective, even where some supply cover, or 'relief teaching' as it is sometimes known, is provided for the teachers involved (Goulden, 1986).

The above goals are summarised in six principles of IT-INSET, which are:

1. observing practice;
2. analysing practice and applying theory (practical theorising);
3. evaluating the curriculum;
4. developing the curriculum;
5. working as a team; and
6. involving the school's other teachers in the process.

(Ashton *et al.*, 1989, p. 9)

IT-INSET at Newman and Westhill Colleges

Colleges began to introduce IT-INSET into their teacher training programmes for special educational needs in the 1980s. Newman and Westhill Colleges, Birmingham, which already had a well established reputation for their special needs work and had made distinctive contributions to the training of teachers of pupils with severe learning difficulties, recognised that IT-INSET could provide a natural extension of their programmes. The Colleges have been responsible for the introduction of IT-INSET into selected mainstream schools, with large numbers of special needs pupils, and into a range of special schools. Over the years the number of special schools involved in the project has increased. In 1990, out of a total of 98 third-year B.Ed. students at Westhill College, 24 have worked in special schools or in mainstream schools with an identified special needs focus. Other students considered special needs issues as part of IT-INSET, but these were not officially recorded.

Table 5.1

Newman Westhill College – IT-INSET 1990 SPECIAL EDUCATION FOCUS				
	Schools	Students	Teachers	Tutors
Mainstream (Primary)	1	4	1	1
Moderate Learning Difficulties (Secondary)	1	4	1	1
Physically Handicapped and Profound and Multiple Learning Difficulties	3	10	3	3
Severe Learning Difficulties	2	6	2	2
TOTAL	7	24	7	7

The benefits of IT-INSET for special needs teachers

Since 1986 the coordinators of IT-INSET have conducted an on-going survey to determine the benefits of the projects for special needs teachers. Although the main comments are summarised below, it must be stressed that this collection of evidence does not constitute a systematic evaluation. The responses, however, are of value in determining future developments, and are consistent with those made by teachers of mainstream children who took part in the National Evaluation of IT-INSET in 1986/87 (Ashton *et al.*, 1989).

Although in the United Kingdom in the 1970s and 80s it was common for teachers to be released for one-year additional (supplementary) training courses, such secondments are now rare, but teachers are often required to attend short courses in school time in order to familiarise themselves with national initiatives. These absences and the consequent disruptions can often disadvantage pupils who desperately need the security of established relationships. In particular, pupils with profound and multiple learning difficulties, who are functioning at a low developmental level, need a consistent approach if any real learning is to take place. Similarly, pupils with challenging behaviour need stability as they can react adversely to teacher absences and to unfamiliar faces. IT-INSET, therefore, is ideal for special needs teachers as it does not involve lengthy absences from the classroom.

One alternative, the system of in-service training based in the school and run by the teachers themselves, was regarded as being too insular and IT-INSET, offering wider perspectives, insight and knowledge, was preferred. Teachers were, however, aware that careful thought was needed in order to avoid the problems which could arise with a team of adults in the classroom. As one teacher put it 'we could be in the position of having more managers than workers!' Teachers also appreciated the value of regular, weekly, IT-INSET as it gave them the time and opportunity to reflect on the work in progress.

Improvement in the quality of education: the national evaluation of IT-INSET

IT-INSET has the advantage of allowing the focus to be on those aspects of the curriculum which a teacher may consider relevant to a specific teaching situation. This freedom to choose is particularly valuable at a time when there is a tendency to place the emphasis on a prescribed curriculum geared to the needs of more able pupils.

Evaluation of the approach in over 20 training institutions and over 30 Local Education Authorities (LEAs) showed that benefits were greatest when there was a match between the principles described above and the teacher education philosophies of the LEA and the training institution. Where this was the case, fruitful partnerships were usually evident. Effective collaboration was characterised by:

- joint clarification of purposes;
- recognition that benefits to the LEA and to training institutions are reciprocal;
- joint overall planning and evaluation;
- joint communication with schools;
- provision of supply cover for teachers involved;
- release of teachers by LEAs to evaluate programmes, and to act as tutors;
- continuing discussions about INSET policy and course developments;
- joint interviewing of applicants for award-bearing INSET courses;
- evaluation of a shared teacher education philosophy.
  (Ashton *et al.*, 1989, p. 156)

Teachers' perceptions of the benefits to themselves were as follows:

- opportunity to work with small groups of children;
- new ideas;
- opportunity to observe children and evaluate learning;
- teamwork/collaboration;
- links with the college;
- opportunity to observe others teaching;
- builds confidence, encourages reflection on teaching;
- opportunity to discuss/exchange ideas/explain ideas;
- curriculum development;
- updating/access to current thinking;
- impetus and enthusiasm;
- extra help;
- enjoyment.
  (Ashton *et al.*, 1989, p. 134)

Teachers also welcomed the opportunity to focus on problems recently encountered as a result of the introduction of the National Curriculum into schools in England and Wales. An impressive example was the invaluable work undertaken in one special school, for pupils with severe learning difficulties, in extending the programmes of study of core areas of the National Curriculum in order to include pupils with severe sensory impairments. In this case, the presence of the IT-INSET team was essential as it provided the extra resources for the teacher to experiment with activities and to critically examine their effectiveness in terms of her pupils' learning. This opportunity to systematically observe children's learning and to record it in exact detail is vital in the development of a professional and critical approach to classroom enquiry. Special needs teachers stressed that IT-INSET provides them with opportunities to articulate and to test their own personal theories in debate with other members of the team.

The review and development of the whole school curriculum

The last of IT-INSET's six principles is to involve other teachers in the school in order that the true potential of IT-INSET can be exploited. If this involvement is fully implemented, the school as a whole will benefit from curriculum innovation, development and renewal. In some schools it has contributed to the development of a 'whole school approach' to many aspects of special needs teaching, and has influenced, for example, the planning of the curriculum, the development of teaching styles and approaches, and the management of children within the classroom and the school.

The benefits of using IT-INSET for special needs training

A recent publication by the National Council for Special Education (1990) provides comprehensive recommendations for the essential content of special needs in-service training courses. It should be stressed that although these recommendations are intended for courses designed for qualified teachers, the material included also has wide implications for the development of pre-service training. The working party identified ten elements essential to a broad and balanced course:

(1) Background Studies
(2) Theory and Philosophy
(3) Assessment Issues
(4) Curriculum Delivery
(5) The Reflective Practitioner
(6) Professional Roles
(7) The Whole School Approach
(8) Personal Development
(9) Management
(10) Exceptional Special Needs

Special needs teachers and students are being asked to comment on whether these ten elements had been included and fully addressed. Initial responses indicate that the majority believe that IT-INSET is an effective approach to the practical component of all the elements, with the obvious exception of 'Background Studies'.

The national evaluation again provides supporting evidence. In its study of the key characteristics of successful teams, the overlap with the essential elements listed above is quite striking. The key characteristics identified were:-

- *discussion* of the philosophy and purpose of IT-INSET; (1), (2)
- *focus* upon a clear issue in the *pupil's learning*; (4), (3)
- joint clarification of the team's focus; (9)
- exchanging the classroom roles to be taken each week by team members; (6)
- taking joint responsibility for planning classroom work; (9)
- planning jointly what and how to observe; (3)
- sharing the teaching; (6), (8)
- making structured observations; (3)
- having an explicit agenda for evaluation meetings; (9), (5)
- rotating the roles of discussion leader and minute taker among all members; (8)
- having the minimum of an hour's team discussion each week; (5)
- analysing pupils' learning; (3)
- raising issues and questions concerning both the pupils' observed learning and the IT-INSET processes of collaborative evaluation and development; (2)
- maintaining the focus on evaluating pupils' learning throughout the programme; (4), (3)
- sharing a common purpose and being equally committed; (7)
- all contributing ideas and being willing to learn from one another;
- being democratic; (9), (7)
  (Ashton *et al.*, 1989, p.168)

(Figures in brackets refer to the relevant essential elements from the National Council for Special Education, 1990). Clearly, therefore, there is consistency between the staff development needs of teachers in special education and the benefits provided by the IT-INSET approach.

Postscript

IT-INSET was first developed in England in 1978 at the Open University with funding from the Department of Education and Science. In 1981 the project moved to the University of Leicester and was established as the Centre for the Evaluation and Development of Teacher Education. DES funding was then extended until 1988 and the Centre was able to employ full-time and part-time staff. A National Evaluation was carried out by the Leicester staff in 1986/1987.

In 1989 the project was moved to two Birmingham Colleges and became the IT-INSET National Network. With the help and support of Birmingham Polytechnic and the Regional Coordinators, who also act as facilitators, the Network provides a basic service for the dissemination and exchange of information and for the supply of advice and practical help.

The 22 British Institutions using IT-INSET report significant increases in the number of students, teachers and tutors involved. In addition, IT-INSET is now being established in Australia, Spain and Malaysia.

References

Ashton, P. M. E., Hunt, P., Jones, S. and Watson, G. (1980) *Curriculum in Action – An Approach to Evaluation*. Milton Keynes: Open University Press.

Ashton, P. M. E., Henderson, E. S. and Peacock, A. (1989) *Teacher Education Through Evaluation: The Principles and Practice of IT-INSET*. London, Routledge Education.

DES (1989) *Initial Teacher Training: Approval of Courses*, Circular No. 24/89. London: DES.

Goulden, R. (1986) *Costs and Benefits: IT-INSET in Calderdale Primary Schools*, CEDTE Occasional paper No. 38. Birmingham: Newman-Westhill Colleges.

Marks, M. and Peacock, D. (1988) 'Teacher Education in a Collaborative Context: Piloting IT-INSET in Australia', *South Pacific Journal Teacher Education*, **16**, 2, 33–42.

Sewell, G. (1987) *The Teacher as Learner: The Whole School Approach – An IT-INSET Programme in Seaton Junior School*, CEDTE Occasional Paper No. 40. Birmingham: Newman-Westhill Colleges.

National Council for Special Education (1990) *Guidelines for the Content of Teachers' Courses in Special Educational Needs*. Stratford: NCSE.

Bibliography

Alexander, R. J. (1984) 'Innovation and Continuity in the Initial Teacher Education Curriculum', in Alexander, R. J., Craft, M. and Lynch, J. (Eds) *Change in Teacher Education: Context and Provision since Robbins*, pp. 103–60. London: Holt, Rinehart and Winston.

Alexander, R., Wilcocks, J. and Kinder, K. (1989) *Changing Primary Practice*. London: Falmer Press.

Ashton, P. M. E., Henderson, E., Merritt, J. and Mortimer, D. (1983) *Teacher Education in the Classroom: Initial and In-Service*. London: Croom Helm.

62

Ashton, P. M. E., Peacock, A. and Preston, M. (1984) *Doing IT-INSET: No. 1. Getting Started*. Birmingham: IT-INSET National Network, Newman and Westhill Colleges.

Booth, M. (1990) *Some Practical Tips for IT-INSET*. Occasional Paper 1 Series 2. Birmingham: IT-INSET National Network, Newman and Westhill Colleges.

Council for the Accreditation of Teacher Education (1986) *Links Between Initial Teacher Training Institutions and Schools*, (CATE Note No. 4). London: CATE.

Everton, T. and Impey, G. (Eds) (1989) *IT-INSET: Partnership in Training. The Leicestershire Experience*. London: David Fulton.

HMI (1989) *A Survey of IT-INSET in Some Leicestershire Schools*. Leicester: University of Leicester.

Marsh, C. (1986) 'IT-INSET: "A panacea for the 1980s?" ', *Journal of Curriculum Studies*, **18**, 4, pp. 449–53.

Sayers, J. and Jones, N. (Eds) (1985) *Teacher Training & Special Educational Needs*. London: Croom Helm.

Tickle, L. (1987) *Learning Teaching, Teaching Teaching. A Study of Partnership in Teacher Education*. London: Falmer Press.

Tilstone, C. (1986) *IT-INSET: Building Productive Working Relationships*. Birmingham: IT-INSET National Network, Newman-Westhill Colleges.

CHAPTER 6

Training Teachers of Children with Special Needs at a Distance

Heather Mason and Carol Miller

The nature of distance-learning

During the last two decades, educational institutions throughout the world have developed distance-taught courses which provide access to learning at many levels. In the United Kingdom distance-learning has become familiar through the work of the Open University, which has served as a model of delivery for many other countries. People who have not had an opportunity to attend a university for a traditionally-taught course have gained degrees and other higher qualifications by working 'at a distance'. This chapter describes how distance-learning is used by teachers to obtain qualifications in special educational needs from The University of Birmingham in England.

Distance-learning, in this case, involves home study through written texts, recordings and other materials which are sent to students by post. Reading therefore is the main medium of study, but the written texts also provide activities which aim to engage students actively with the ideas presented and to give them practical tasks to carry out in their work contexts. There is a difference between this type of education and that provided by more traditional 'correspondence' courses and the now rapidly-developing 'open-learning' approaches. In both of these, there is often an amount of flexibility of starting and finishing times of courses for the student. Most open-learning systems allow the pace of learning to be determined by the student and there may be a wide variety of choice of learning topics and outcomes allowed. The specialist distance-taught courses at Birmingham, at least for the moment, have less flexibility. All students begin and end at the same time, covering a pre-set syllabus. Within the syllabus there will be some opportunity for choice, according to the requirements of the student's particular work needs so that, for example, activities will vary and there may be a choice of assignments. The assessment of the course, however, conforms to university standards and leads to the award of a recognised diploma or degree.

In addition to the materials sent out to students, there is an important 'live' element in the learning. All of the distance-learning courses incorporate two, one-week, residential summer schools at the University, when practical and experiential work takes place and students have an important opportunity to meet with each other and with the staff of the University. Sessions are designed to build upon the information already presented and to introduce areas which are of either specific or general interest. Whilst there is a busy scheduled timetable for the week, about a third of the time is left 'free' for students to use libraries and to talk to each other. Course evaluation shows that this is seen as a vital part of the courses. The other 'live' component of the courses is the contact with tutors at other times. The particular systems employed will be described below but the contact with University or local tutors in both cases constitutes a crucial element of support for students in potentially isolated and anxious situations. Telephone contact is essential and the encouragement of a student-contact network is important. This often develops following a successful summer school if tutors have effectively facilitated the social as well as the academic curriculum during that week.

The materials which form the core of the courses are prepared by the University staff or by other experienced people in the specialism who are commissioned to write texts which are then edited at the University. Preparation of material in an appropriate style which is interesting and comprehensible to students reading at home requires skills which may be different from those used when teaching a class or when writing for other purposes. So-called 'interactive text' in a personalised style is required, where students are addressed as 'you' and frequent reference is made to other parts of the course to link ideas and to help students' comprehension (Holmberg, 1989). A critical difference between this type of course and a more traditional, taught course is that topics are necessarily taught sequentially, rather than concurrently. Subjects do not so easily 'feed in' to each other and there are no opportunities to stop a tutor and to ask for clarification of a point. The lay-out of text will affect its attractiveness. Developments in desktop publishing are influencing this, allowing the use of graphics to 'brighten up' the page and to focus attention at certain points.

The advantages and disadvantages of distance- and open-learning have been widely documented (Jevons, 1984; 1988). This chapter therefore, examines those which apply directly to mature students following training courses at The University of Birmingham in the area of special needs and suggests ways in which the model may be applied to a much larger target group.

For many mature students, one of the main advantages of distance-learning is the accessibility to higher educational courses which are not available at a university close to their home. An added advantage is that they do not have to leave their home area and family to attend a full-time course at the University or to leave their paid employment. Whilst this has obvious benefits for the student with financial commitments, a family or elderly relatives, there is increasing evidence to suggest that it is not only those students with domestic commitments who welcome this pattern of study (Kelly, 1988) but also those students who have a highly organised and active social life within their local community.

A policy of the full-time distance-learning courses is to accept only students already working in their chosen field of study. These students therefore have the advantage of learning or updating skills and knowledge and being able to put theory into practice on a daily basis, with the added advantage of being surrounded by experienced teachers working in a similar area. This is not always the case with university-based courses at Birmingham, which often attract teachers who have not necessarily taught children with a specific special need before but are seeking further training in order to change direction in their career. Whilst such a course allows a total immersion in their studies there is only a limited time for face-to-face contact with the children.

One of the problems of a relatively low-incidence disability such as visual impairment or speech and language difficulties in any country is that the numbers of teachers who may require training can fluctuate from year to year which can mean that it would not be viable for courses to start up in other areas of a country to cater for short-term needs. In addition the potential student population will always have a wide geographical spread, which in turn makes attendance at a local campus impossible. Distance-learning allows training institutions to target these students easily and to respond to any local and national changes quickly and efficiently. It can also cater for the needs of countries which are too small to sustain a specific course but who may share similar language and cultural identities with a larger one.

Experience in Britain has shown that many of the students attending university on a full-time course do not necessarily go back to the position from which they were released in order to take the higher qualification, but instead use the year to re-assess their career opportunities, perhaps ending up with promotion within another area of the country. It would appear that distance-learning students are likely to be more cost-effective since experience has indicated that they tend to stay in the same post immediately after qualifying, giving stability to the school or service. It is also unusual for these students to change jobs during training as this would have major implications for the payment of fees.

Whilst a student and his or her employer may appreciate the access to higher education which distance-learning provides, there is still the problem of fitting studies and, for some courses, teaching placements away from home, alongside a full-time job with possibly demanding family circumstances. Although some schools and colleges attempt to give the student study time during the week, this is not always possible on a regular basis and indeed, in the speech and language course, it is extremely rare. Added to this, the student is then expected to attend the annual summer school, which in some cases falls in their vacation, and to commit themselves to other regular seminars held in their region throughout the year. As two of these courses lead to a mandatory qualification (in England and Wales, teachers of classes of children with a visual or hearing impairment must undergo a recognised training course within three years of being appointed to a post) the question of choice does not enter the discussions with other members of the family, who may be affected by the absence from home. There is also the threat for some students that failure to complete the course or pass all the relevant parts may result in dismissal from their job.

On a professional level, students learning at a distance do not have the same access to campus-based resources: for example, the specialist collections of books and professional journals, the immediate access to tutors face-to-face (although every effort is made for easy access via the telephone). If time can be considered a personal resource of full-time students, then the luxury of being able to discuss and argue with fellow students following a wide range of courses in special needs is not available to them. To compensate for this, students are encouraged to form self-help and interest groups either on a regional basis or on a national basis if they are working in a highly specialised field, for example with the deaf/blind population.

One of the criticisms of distance-learning courses is that although they are highly suitable for passing on ideas and information, there is a question mark over their ability to teach practical skills (Best, 1989). Best also argues that courses often need to change attitudes and that there is some doubt that this can be achieved through distance-learning. However, one has to balance the argument with the point of view that these are experienced teachers receiving 'on the job' training and the fact that many have voluntarily applied to come on the course shows a certain commitment to the idea of change. Many will have a far greater opportunity to practise skills which some believe can only be achieved through full-time training. It needs to be remembered too that campus-based students inevitably have more limited access to children. Experience has indicated that attitude-change is not necessarily related to the mode of course delivery.

Distance-learning courses for teachers of children with special educational needs

Training to teach children with special educational needs in the UK is undertaken at post-basic qualification level. That is, qualified teachers with experience in mainstream education may choose to develop their career in a particular area of special education. Whilst there is increasing emphasis on the integration of all children into ordinary schools, there is, nevertheless a need for teachers to understand specific educational difficulties arising from say, sensory or motor problems or from learning difficulties.

In the case of children with visual or auditory impairment, as has already been stated, teachers are required by the Department of Education and Science to obtain a specialist qualification and, until recently, these particular special educational needs were designated as national priorities for training, with special financial allocations. For other types of special need, for example severe communication difficulties, teachers are not required to obtain a specialist qualification. However, the increasing number of units and classes opening for children with speech and language disorders have served to raise awareness that special knowledge is essential for this work. Teachers have expressed a need for training and the distance-learning course at The University of Birmingham has been developed, based on the expressed needs of teachers in the field. Teachers with such understanding are then able to support children with special needs in the mainstream setting or to work in special schools which provide resources for particular handicapping conditions. The specialist training for teachers is often undertaken at a stage when they are becoming well established in their teaching career and frequently have family and other commitments. Distance-education presents a practical and economical means of continuing professional development for mature learners who have made a choice to become specialist teachers. This is consistent with Chung's (1990) view that the realities of distance-education make it an important contributor to individual and personal satisfaction and to social mobility in industrialised countries.

At the University of Birmingham, specialist distance-learning courses have been developed for teachers of children with visual impairment, hearing impairment and for those with speech and language disorders. The courses are based in the School of Education in a traditional, campus university. The School has a large special educational needs section and has long experience of offering campus-based courses in visual impairment and in hearing impairment as well as in other areas of special education. The distance-taught courses are offered at post-graduate diploma and at degree levels and are designed to conform to the modular structure of all of the courses in the School of Education at Birmingham. This provides the students with the same opportunities as those who are campus-based to pursue higher degrees and to undertake research later if they wish.

Whilst the courses are equivalent in standard and in outcome to campus-based courses, there are very specific issues relating to the instigation of distance-taught courses. Distance-learning may provide an economical form of training, but the experience of setting up and developing the special education courses at the University of Birmingham has shown that there is no cheap short cut to the initial stages. Materials used to teach students on campus do not transfer to the distance system. Indeed, staff involved in campus-teaching do not always adapt readily to distance-teaching and may not be sympathetic to the particular needs of the students. They will rarely have the time required and may not be available at the unsocial hours expected of distance-learning students. Teaching materials are required, specifically designed for the needs of students who may be working alone, away from libraries and bookshops. However, colleagues who have become involved in the preparation of distance-learning materials report that as a consequence they have reviewed their regular teaching with considerable benefit. Time and money are essential if distance courses of quality are to be prepared.

The main elements of the distance-learning courses for special education teachers consist of sequential and inter-related units, making up five core modules. The units are presented via texts and recordings which are sent to students for home study over a period of two years. Activities within the materials are designed to engage the students and to enhance their understanding of theoretical concepts. Since, in order to qualify for acceptance on the courses, students must already be working in their chosen specialism, they have access to 'live' examples and classroom situations which serve as illustrative examples for the linking of theory to practice and through which students can evaluate their learning. Each module is assessed through an assignment in the form of a written report, an essay or a recording. A sixth module in all of the courses comprises a work-related project in which the student undertakes a small piece of classroom-based research. Careful design of activities and guidance in selection of projects can ensure that distance-learning can be effective in developing students' practical abilities as well as their theoretical knowledge.

Despite all the efforts made by the institution, one of the major disadvantages of any distance-learning course is the sense of isolation and insecurity felt by the students at certain times. These feelings may be related to the pressure of the work or, as with any students, are of a personal nature and are exacerbated by not being able to discuss course work with fellow students or course tutors on a day-to-day basis. The structure of the various distance courses allows for different methods to overcome this problem, for example, a system of personal tutors.

There is no doubt that students learning at a distance may miss opportunities to participate in practical group work. There is no guarantee that all of the students will have access to the same specialist equipment which would be necessary, for example, for the assessment of vision or the testing of hearing. Day-to-day contact with similarly-motivated colleagues can be important for special education teachers who may work in relatively isolated situations if they are the only specialist in an ordinary school. For these reasons, the summer schools and the locally-based tutorials and seminars are particularly important. Whilst the details of the tutoring system varies, the need for students to have personal contact with each other and with a tutor is recognised in each of the courses. In the course for teachers of children with visually impairment, the staff of the University organise seminars in different parts of the country for the students. In addition, each student is guided and assessed in their practical teaching by a supervisor experienced in work with visually handicapped children. The course in hearing impairment also has periods of assessed teaching practice, supervised by course staff and by experienced teachers in the field. In the courses on hearing impairment and speech and language disorders, students are allocated to tutorial groups which meet at intervals throughout the year. Robinson (1981) has outlined the role of so-called 'educational counsellors' in distance education. These experienced professionals support the students at tutorial meetings and between-times through telephone discussions and correspondence. Tutors are also involved in the marking of students' assignments in cooperation with staff of the University. In the course on language disorder, a support system has been organised to help the tutors' development. Tutors are paired. The pair exchange students' work for double-marking and are available to each other for discussion. Feedback on this system indicates that some of the anxieties of tutors can be allayed by providing an opportunity for them to talk to a colleague. Training days are arranged for the tutors at the University and there are frequent opportunities for other contact with the University staff. It should also be said that with three distance-learning courses now running in the School of Education at Birmingham, meetings of the University staff involved help to provide the essential support for them, working as they do in a system providing more conventional courses where colleagues do not always understand the nature of distance-teaching.

The way forward

Many possibilities are offered through distance-learning. There is increasing awareness that traditional approaches to education and training are not necessarily the best means of economically providing outcomes of quality. The models described above can be used in a number of settings, adapting them to local needs. Where cost is of primary concern, provided the means are available for initial setting up of courses, distance-education 'can offer a lower-cost form of education where the financing of large-scale education programs is often seriously problematic' (Chung, 1990, p. 61). Examples of teacher training by distance-education can be found in Somalia (Hadi Said, 1990) and in Papua New Guinea (Simpson, 1990). Developments in Europe are leading to reciprocal recognition of qualifications from member states. There are many possibilities for the use of distance-education in this context.

Finally, it can not be denied that the potential flexibility for meeting training needs is one of the most exciting aspects of these distance-learning courses. By 'mixing and matching' modules from all the courses and by allowing alternative time schedules for their completion, training packages for a wide spectrum of professionals could be provided, tailored to individual or group needs. In the UK, classroom assistants form a vital element of the educational workforce whose training needs have been severely neglected. Distance-learning approaches might be used to enhance their skills and confidence flexibly and economically. The possibilities are numerous for any professionals who wish to continue their education and keep up with developments in their field when they are not in a position to attend courses in the traditional way.

References

Best, A. B. (1989) 'Distance Education for Teachers of Visually Handicapped Students', *Journal of Visual Impairment and Blindness*, **83**, 1, 76–80.

Chung, F. (1990) 'Strategies for Developing Distance Education', in Croft, M., Mugridge, I., Daniel, J. S. and Hershfield, A. (Eds) *Distance Education: Development and Access*. Caracas, Venezuela: International Council for Distance Education.

Hadi Said, A. (1990) 'Distance Education in Somalia: An Emergency Program of Teacher Training', in Croft, M., Mugridge, I., Daniel, J. S. and Hershfield, A. (Eds) *Distance Education: Development and Access*. Caracas, Venezuela: International Council for Distance Education.

Holmberg, B. (1989) *Theory and Practice of Distance Education*. London: Routledge.

Jevons, F. R. (1984) 'Distance Education in a Mixed Institution: Working Towards Parity', *Distance Education*, **5**, 1, 24–37.

Jevons, F. R. (1988) 'Parity of Esteem', in Smith, P. and Kelly, M. E. (Eds) *Distance Education and the Mainstream*. London: Croom Helm.

Kelly, M. E. (1988) 'Barriers to Convergence in Australian Higher Education', in Smith, P. and Kelly, M. E. (Eds) *Distance Education and the Mainstream*. London: Croom Helm.

Robinson, B. (1981) 'Support for Student Learning', in Kaye, A. and Rumble, G. (Eds) *Distance Teaching for Higher and Adult Education*. London: Croom Helm.

Simpson, N. L. (1990) 'Combining Distance Education with Residential Instruction to Upgrade Secondary Teachers in Papua New Guinea', in Croft, M., Mugridge, I., Daniel, J. S. and Hershfield, A. (Eds) *Distance Education: Development and Access*. Caracas, Venezuela: International Council for Distance Education.

CHAPTER 7

The Facilitator's Role in Action Research for Teachers of Pupils with Special Educational Needs

Christine O'Hanlon

The professional development of teachers forms the main role of the in-service department in the Education Faculty of a university, polytechnic or college. The department members all share a similar purpose which is to offer every course applicant a chance to become a better professional, a better teacher and member of a school community. The university where I am based has accepted these aims for a number of years. However, the way of developing these simple aims has changed in recent years, through the focus on action research in the professional development of teachers of pupils with special educational needs.

Action research is educational research which actively involves teachers in curriculum development through a process of professional development. The main focus of action research is to encourage teachers to view themselves as active researchers of their own practice. Action research as a term is associated with Kurt Lewin (1946), and has been advanced in educational contexts internationally since then by Schon (1983), Corey (1953) and Carr and Kemmis (1986) among many others. Action research in the United Kingdom is usually associated with Lawrence Stenhouse (1975) whose ideas were elaborated through a process model of curriculum development rather than an objectives model. The process model of curriculum development emphasised a mediation of the practice of teaching and the assumptions about knowledge which formed the foundations of teaching. Stenhouse's principles were put into action in the Humanities Project in Cambridgeshire in the late 1960s when teachers were encouraged to collect classroom data for use in formulating hypotheses for testing different teaching strategies. The significant factor about the notion of the teacher as researcher being put into practice in this way is that teachers in this project were encouraged to work together in groups and to share data and collaborate in the generation of hypotheses. Teachers were not working individually in their classroom research, they were collaborating with each other and sharing their professional problems and concerns. Elliott (1986) claims that this enterprise 'was linked with a process model of curriculum which posited curriculum and teacher development as one and the same enterprise'. He continues to describe this development of action research as a cyclical process 'within the terms of which model teachers develop the curriculum and themselves through cycles of action research – of reflection upon action followed by action upon reflection'.

As professionals who develop teachers of pupils with special educational needs in the professional context, how then do we develop teachers and the curriculum within the same framework? How do we develop teachers through the curriculum in the cycle of action research? As teacher trainers or as in-service tutors we engage in the professional development of teachers through a process of action research. Within the institutional framework for professional development there is the opportunity for discrete groups of teachers of pupils with special educational needs in the ordinary and the special school, in units or any other setting, to research and improve their practice. Through the cyclical and flexible process of action research, changes are initiated and monitored in complex social situations in schools and evolve into plans for action within which those involved learn from their own experience. The final outcome is to enable individuals and groups of people to organise the conditions under which they can learn from their own experience and make their understanding accessible to others. Within this framework, professionals who work in an educational context can change their environment and conditions through self-awareness and deliberate action for curriculum improvement. Teachers of pupils with special educational needs are professionals who participate in this process of curriculum improvement.

Action research can be seen as a form of self evaluation, self analysis and redirection; it may in fact be seen as a psychodynamic process where a tutor supports a teacher through a new learning procedure, to produce better professionals through a process of continual renewal. This process of continual renewal depends on the skills and expertise of the managers, coordinators, consultants or facilitators. The name 'facilitator' is now often used for tutors who formerly lectured and imparted wisdom to their students, to indicate a change in focus. A facilitator is a person who eases the action or performance for another. This definition implies a change in role from the transmission model to the support model of teaching. As a facilitator of professionals I act as a support tutor for teachers engaging in their own professional re-evaluation. With this change in nomenclature I believe that I am:

(1) Enhancing professional development and improving the educational experiences of children and professionals.
(2) Exposing professional to a range of concepts, theories and models of knowledge which are appropriate to the clarification and resolution of their problems and issues.
(3) Developing the professionals' research skills, and subsequently improving their ability to articulate and further develop coherent theories and practices.
(4) Establishing in professionals a capacity for professional renewal which will continue for their professional careers.
(5) Enabling professionals to evaluate and to respond constructively to the issues which they encounter in practice, including both practical and policy issues.
(6) Enabling professionals to become more effective members of their professional community.

I am encouraging a more autonomous, self-reflective role for the professionals in their everyday practice than formerly. I am moving from a position of developing in my students the philosophy of knowledge to a position of the philosophy of wisdom (Maxwell, 1984). I no longer present knowledge and information for the student's consumption. Instead I am helping to instil intention and action into their professional lives so that they may discover and perform those actions which enable them to realise what is of value in life (Elliott, 1990). This may be realised through the combination of knowledge and wisdom; i.e. the production of knowledge which rests upon the rational inquiry of actions which leads to greater insight into the basic values within professional practice.

    Action research combines these two forms of intellectual inquiry. Every person possesses fundamental knowledge which can be developed through education and schooling. This knowledge plays an important role in supporting the fundamental process of practical inquiry. In undertaking action research the professional searches for particular knowledge or facts in order to fill in the background for the issue or problem which is being investigated. Decisions are made about what facts need to be uncovered or clarified to start the action research process; this process is repeated again during the further development of the action research cycle. As it is impossible to solve a complex problem or resolve a complex issue without deliberation and the elucidation of pertinent facts and data, the evolution of satisfactory situations therefore involves an analysis of the practical problem into a number of subordinate problems of knowledge. It is through this process that the professionals' values are actualised in practice.

Professional and personal values are difficult to differentiate in practice. The professional involved in the process of inquiry holds distinct and individual personal values, values which are brought to bear daily on the individual's own attempts to solve 'life' issues in the world. The realisation of personal or professional values becomes clear through the person's attempts to solve the complex problems associated with the education of pupils with special educational needs. Elliott (1990) sees the importance of a person's own values in investigation and inquiry, and stresses their importance in developing knowledge: 'Value bias is a necessary condition of useful knowledge'.

De Bono (1976) also stresses the importance of values in the informing of thinking and action. He writes that: 'Values determine thinking and the acceptability of the result'. Therefore in my efforts to ease the professional into a position of becoming 'wise' I must acknowledge each person's particular bias and prejudice within the process of researching his or her practice. I must appreciate individual professional values and learn to know them rather than attempt to change them immediately. I try to find ways to enable the professional to detect the influences of his or her values on practical working situations with pupils in schools and units.

What is the facilitator's role?

Within the institution, the facilitator is the class or unit tutor who is responsible for undertaking the professional development of the participants within an award-bearing context. The role is implicitly a fostering of the professional's development in different educational contexts, for example, a remedial teacher in a secondary school or a teacher in a special school. Teachers and professionals engaged in all forms of education are involved. Both primary and secondary level teachers, ordinary and specialist teachers all share data and collaborate. The tutor's role is varied and complex; it comprises:

Practical Role

(1) Defining an issue or concern for investigation.
(2) Selecting, preparing and evaluating research methods and means.
(3) Defining the unit aims, product and timescale.
(4) Writing the unit syllabus for institutional validation.
(5) Studying and preparing relevant reading and theories.
(6) Discussion and reflection on the unit focus and the educational concerns related to it.
(7) Organising the practical aspects of research activities.
(8) Organising the group discussion and learning.
(9) Preparing materials and executing tutorial materials.
(10) Guiding the learning processes of participants.
(11) Conducting the unit product/case study assessment.
(12) Conducting the students' evaluation of the unit.

These aspects comprise the practical role of organising and teaching the action research unit. However, there are other aspects of the facilitator's role which are more esoteric and I will refer to them within the supporting, inspirational role.

Inspirational Role

(1) Creating an open trusting environment to enable good group communication.
(2) Negotiating an informal 'learning contract' between tutor and professional.
(3) Operating with impartiality and neutrality in a value-laden situation.
(4) Coping with anxiety and stress projected by professionals undertaking action research for professional improvement.
(5) Helping the professional to develop negotiation skills for the collection of sensitive data.
(6) Organising and choosing the methods and means of group cohesion.
(7) Reformulating and discussing values implicit in the group processes.

The practical and the inspirational role make different demands on the facilitator. The practical role with its twelve factors can be planned and managed ahead of time. This role can also be considered to be similar in the various factors to the tutor's traditional role. In this sense the institutional tutor who is learning to become a facilitator, 'knows the ropes' already. S/he has experienced the organisation for the practice of tutoring course units for a more traditional transmission model. The practical role has been practised and learned. However, the inspirational role, the immediate skills described above in seven statements, requires the tutor to engage in new learning procedures. S/he must now become a democratic teacher, that is, s/he must foster the autonomy and confidence of the students. S/he must now 'enable' the professionals through a process of open communication.

The tutor maintains a directing role which may not be a 'controlling' role. The teachers/participants all share in the control of the group. The group progressively develops its autonomy during the unit. However, the tutor as a facilitator is also a participant in the group communication. This may mean that the tutor's role will be undertaken by all the participants from time to time, that is, the responsibility for fostering and maintaining open communication in a trusting environment may fall on all members on occasions. Each participant's role in the action research process must be clear to them and they must also make known their understanding of the role to others if democratic relations are to be maintained. Jansen and Mallekoote (1989) found that role definition was valuable in action research projects. They write that: 'Democratic procedures and emancipatory aims cannot be strived for if the roles different people play in a project are hidden, and if open communication on these matters is lacking'.

The participants' role in the group discussion during the unit must also be clear. The roles of participants need to be negotiated and tested in practice. The development of a new role for the university tutor and the fostering of teacher autonomy in this context is very threatening to institutionalised roles, particularly within a traditional lecturer context. This means that the emergent facilitator's role in a university, polytechnic or college context may be problematic. It is the emergence of the institutionalisation of the professional process of action research itself that may be problematic. Holly (1984) refers to the dialectical tension between action research and institutions:

> Action research fosters collegiality (albeit within what are usually small groups), informality, openness and collaboration across boundaries, etc. while institutions veer towards the hierarchical, bureaucratic and formal. Action research when it is a marginal (even temporary) activity may receive institutional toleration; its products – as opposed to its process – can be accommodated as long as this separate process (that of institutionalisation...) is conducted under the institution's surveillance.

In the university faculty where I was recently engaged as a facilitator on the In-Service B.Ed (Hons) (Professional Development), the action research process is confined to a small number of 'convicted' tutors. The university surveillance consists of rigorous course validation procedures, and exacting internal and external course/unit assessment procedures. Each unit on the B.Ed obliges each participant to produce a product: an assignment of approximately 3,000 words outlining and describing the action research process in relation to his or her investigation and his or her attempts to improve a particular professional area. There are four units undertaken by participants or candidates in each year. Two units address the practice of action research itself, while another two units focus directly on special needs issues, for example the identification of pupils with special educational needs or the integration of pupils with special educational needs into the ordinary school. The assessment criteria for each unit are carefully pre-determined and validated by the institution and are as follows:

> Each candidate should be able to use the literature eclectically to illuminate and extend his/her understanding of the problems and issues, and to demonstrate his/her grasp of the relevant knowledge, theories, concepts and models in the field. Evidence indicating the degree to which the candidate has understood the theories, concepts, techniques and models encountered will be sought in terms of his/her ability to explain and to use them in the course of both conducting and reporting the research. Such evidence would include an indication of the clarification of initial ideas and concepts, of the qualitative changes in these, and of his/her ability to critically evaluate the literature in terms of the concepts articulated and refined through the research and his/her ability to select and to competently use appropriate research (B.Ed course document, University of Ulster, 1988).

The institution places a heavy emphasis on theories, concepts and models and on the use, selection and evaluation of literature. Each candidate is required to demonstrate competence in selecting and using a range of specified research methods, and in analysing the evidence collected. More specifically the institutional assessment will look for evidence of the candidate's competence in the following variety of approaches to problem solving:

- systematic and accurate observation;
- sensitive and effective interviewing;
- efficient tape recording and selective transcribing;
- comprehensive acquisition of documentary evidence;

- systematic record keeping (diary writing, pupil profiles, analytic memos);
- gaining access to, validating, and negotiating release of institutional information;
- constructing and administering questionnaires;
- triangulation of data.

In addition, the candidate's competence in critically analysing research evidence will be sought through his/her ability to:

- clarify problematic situations in terms of their inherent issues, dilemmas and paradoxes;
- conceptualise conflicting and discrepant data;
- assess situations from a number of different points of view.

The participants or candidates are required to meet the above criteria each year in different and more comprehensive professional contexts.

In Year 1, the investigation focuses on the individual's professional practice in the school situation. In Year 2, the focus is extended to the wider institutional and national context. Year 3 requires candidates to focus on both these and, additionally, to demonstrate an increased competence to carry out a substantial, supervised investigation.

The action research process is institutionalised through the regulations governing student assessment and the overall university procedures for course validation. Action research becomes controlled and moulded. There is a timescale which tutors and participants (professionals) must adhere to. There is a specific product at the completion of a set course of study and investigation which must be assessed within university regulations. There is a distortion in this process. Professionals are drawn in one direction by their action research and in another by their institutions. There is often a mismatch between what professionals are actually doing in their practice and what they say they are doing. There is a tension between their value system and their real practices. The ability to write well, describe, explain, analyse and become reflexive in print is the real secret of success in institutionalised action research assignments. What the professionals actually do in reality is not open to scrutiny; it is only their oral or written reports on their efforts to improve their practice that are subject to group and tutor analysis (see Carr, 1982). Apart from the organisational constraints laid down by educational institutions there are personal and individual constraints within each tutor in facilitating the action research process. There is the danger of stifling the professional process by engaging in learned practices of institutional control.

Elliott (1983) warns us of the propensity to distortion in our own practice.

> Facilitators of teacher based action research need to be constantly deliberating about their own practice and its relationship to the nature of the activity they are trying to facilitate. If they don't engage in this kind of second-order action research they will succumb to pressures to control teachers' thinking, and thereby distort rather than enable the processes of first-order action research (p. 40).

The institutional facilitator is supporting the professionals in carrying out a form of first-order action research with pupils with special needs in schools. It is the enrolled professionals who primarily engaged in research and are carrying out the investigations and making changes in their practices. However, the tutor who facilitates the process is primarily in control of the process and the collaborative discussion through his or her institutional position; the facilitator is allowed to control and direct the institutional discussion and discourse related to the professionals' action research. The facilitator influences the professional process of action research. Therefore the tutor, in order to maintain a neutral position, must be aware of, and investigate his or her own facilitation practices, in order to become conscious of his or her own distortions and biases. The personal and professional values of the facilitator form part of the discourse, therefore his or her influences should be identified. The facilitator should find the situation an opportunity to reflect on his or her own values in education through the practice of supporting the professional development of teachers of pupils with special educational needs. The values of action research are problematic in action research practice just as educational values are problematic in educational practice. Facilitators of action research must conduct action research into their fostering of professional action research just as their students conduct action research into their educational and professional practice. Altrichter (1986) in a case study in action research of professional development in higher education stresses the importance of demonstrating the understanding of a process criteria with a teacher at an early stage in the action research process. He advises both tutor and teacher to reconstruct how agreements are reached and how decisions are brought about. The facilitator could demonstrate his or her understanding of process criteria such as 'balanced communication between teacher and tutor' and 'teacher control over decisions concerning research and action' to illustrate the meaning of such criteria to the teacher and to give the teacher the experience of evaluating these critera.

Any deliberation on the role of the facilitator must recognise that most kinds of facilitation actually foster dependence. This is potentially a contradictory notion within the advocacy of action research, which aspires to free teachers, students, principals, university tutors, researchers and other professionals concerned with the education of pupils with special educational needs from the dictates of tradition, habit and unexamined ideology. How can tutors as facilitators encourage emancipatory practices within their own institutions?

McTaggart and Singh (1987) have debated this issue and suggest an abandoning of the facilitator's role in favour of a more general thinking about the role of groups of 'intellectuals' in fostering social change. They write that:

> In fourth generation action research action researchers would no longer serve as facilitators of critical processes for others. So called facilitators will simply *participate* as organic intellectuals in critical communities struggling for emancipation, guided by a critical consciousness and a systematic and practical sense of critique.

This view is an idealised vision of what we are capable of achieving in our efforts to create communities of professionals engaged in action research. In an equal partnership with our colleagues and other professionals in education and teaching we must simply participate in the same process. We must learn to share our own research and investigation, our reflections and actions within our particular educational group or community. The community may exist already within the field of special needs or it may exist in the broader international educational community. There are action research networks like CARN (Classroom Action Research Network) in the United Kingdom. The community of interest in action research already exists, and action researchers are members of many professional and research associations. Action researchers can help communities of interest in special needs to become self-conscious and critical. Action research in educational institutions can transform the community life of the institution, if there is a commitment to action. In this way it is possible to loosen the grip of technical rationality (Schon, 1983) on professional and educational thinking in the field of special needs.

References

Altrichter, H. (1986) 'Professional Development in Higher Education by Means of Action Research into One's Own Teaching – A Case Study', in *Collaborative Action Research*, Bulletin No. 7. Cambridge: Classroom Action Research Network.

B.Ed Course Committee, (1988) 'Bachelor of Education (Honours) (Professional Development) Course Document'. Jordanstown: Faculty of Education, University of Ulster.

Carr, W. (1982) 'Adapting a Curriculum Philosophy', *Australian Journal of Teaching Practice*, 1, 1.

Carr, W. and Kemmis, S. (1986) *Becoming Critical: Education, Knowledge and Action Research*. London: Falmer Press.

Corey, S. (1953) 'Action Research To Improve School Practices'. New York: Columbia University.

De Bono, E. (1976) *Thinking Action*. Direct Educational Services Ltd, The Friary Press.

Elliott, J. (1983) *Facilitating Action Research from Outside the School*. Cambridge: Institute of Education.

Elliott, J. (1986) 'Teachers as Researchers', in *International Encyclopaedia of Teaching and Teacher Education*. Oxford: Pergamon Press.

Elliott, J. (1990) 'Educational Research in Crisis; Performance indicators and the decline in excellence. BERA Presidential Address', *British Educational Research Journal*, 16, 1, pp. 3–19.

Holly, P. (1984) 'Action Research: A Cautionary Note?', in Holly, P. and Whitehead, D. (Eds), *Action Research in Schools; Getting it into Perspective*, CARN Bulletin No. 6. Classroom Action Research Network.

Jansen, B. and Mallekoote, M. (1989) 'Roles in Action Research', in Owens, P. and Edwards, A. (Eds), *Partnership in Teacher Research*, CARN Bulletin No. 9B. Classroom Action Research Network.

Lewin, K. (1946) 'Action Research and Minority Problems', *Journal of Social Issues*, 2.

McTaggart, R. and Singh, M. (1987) 'A Fourth Generation of Action Research', notes on the Deakin Seminar Educational Research Association Conference, New Orleans.

Maxwell, N. C. (1984) *From Knowledge to Wisdom; A Revolution in the Aims and Methods of Science*. Oxford: Blackwell.

Schon, D. A. (1983) *The Reflective Practitioner: How Professionals Think in Action*. New York: Basic Books.

Stenhouse, L. (1975) *Introduction to Curriculum Research and Development*. Oxford: Heinemann Education.

CHAPTER 8

A School-based In-service Response to Staff Development

Gerda Hanko

Introduction

There is an increasing demand for school-based help for teachers to meet the special needs of their hardest-to-teach and neediest pupils. Current legislation has been adding to the urgency of these demands in Britain. Teachers in other parts of the world are involved in similar debates, while in some countries – such as in the newly liberated east European ones – teachers are only now being asked to meet the needs of pupils burdened with problems which the recently ousted regimes had not allowed to surface and therefore never permitted their teachers to address.

This chapter takes account of the in-service needs of both teachers and special needs specialists faced with teaching children whose needs they feel ill-equipped to meet on their own or even fully understand. It discusses the development of joint problem-solving staff development initiatives, designed to meet pupils' special behavioural, emotional and learning needs while also meeting the teachers' needs: to deepen understanding of such special needs and their interactional aspects, and to develop their abilities to meet them within the ordinary teaching day, through the learning programme, teacher-pupil and classroom relationships, the involvement of fellow professionals within and across schools and school services, and of the children's parents.

Development and discussion

Amongst the fundamental questions raised in the introductory chapter
to this book are the low proportion of teachers who have received any
special training in meeting children's special needs; its necessity or
degree of importance; and the much larger group of teachers we now
acknowledge as being in contact with children with special needs. If we
include in these the many children perceived as 'difficult-to-teach', and
if we accept that 'the skills and qualities required to meet most of the
needs described as special, are those which are desirable in any good
teacher for any pupils' (Sayer, 1987), we have to conclude that all
teachers need to be enabled to be 'good enough' teachers for all their
pupils. And if we accept this conclusion, we need to consider what
modes of delivery might get us there.

My task here is to discuss the principles and practice of a school-
based consultative case discussion model of exploration within a
problem-solving framework, designed to enable teachers to find their
own workable alternative solutions to the problems they face in their
classrooms. The model addresses the stipulation that children with
special emotional, behavioural and learning difficulties in ordinary
schools are the responsibility of the whole school; and that therefore
all teachers need to be supported to be able to accept that responsibility.

Reviewers and evaluators of this approach have commented upon
its potential as a 'model for the development of in-service support
systems' in general (Bowman, 1986); that it demonstrates 'how
ordinary school subjects may be taught in such a way as to assist
children to understanding and handling their problems' (Adams,
1986); shows how it 'can elicit teachers' own hidden "therapeutic"
skills . . . providing children with truly re-educative challenges
embedded in their work at school' (Deveson, 1986); and illustrates
'how even for those whose behaviour reflects difficult circumstances
outside our sphere of influence, a sensitive "curricular" response can
not only have a beneficial effect upon the child for whom it was
intended, but (can) enhance the curriculum for the whole class', as
teachers learn to perceive the challenge of problem behaviour 'not as a
debilitating drain on our resources (but) as an opportunity for us as
teachers to use our skills and professional judgements creatively, and
find solutions which can improve learning opportunities for all'
(Mongon and Hart, 1989).

Helping teachers to *experience* how tackling their difficulties with 'difficult-to-teach pupils' need not be seen as grit in the machine but as part of the job *and* an opportunity for all their other pupils is clearly a challenge at any time. It is crucial now as pupils' increasing difficulties more than ever are raising awareness of their need to have access to that 'broad, balanced curriculum relevant to individual needs' which in Britain the National Curriculum Council (1989a) underlines as their entitlement, requiring teachers to address 'those within-school factors which can prevent or exacerbate some pupils' difficulties'.

Teachers, now especially, must understand, as Mittler (1990) wrote, that for pupils with emotional and behavioural difficulties the problem is 'not one of access to the curriculum alone but of the response of the school as a whole to the diversity of children's behaviour and needs'; they must understand that such children need teachers who 'aim to raise low morale and damaged self-esteem AS MUCH AS academic attainment', and see to it that they are helped as teachers, through the right kind of in-service provision, to develop 'both preventive and interventive strategies relevant to pupils with emotional and behavioural difficulties'.

This complements the recommendations made by the Committee of Enquiry on Discipline in Schools (the Elton Committee; Department of Education and Science, 1989) to help teachers become better classroom *managers* and to develop *school-based teacher support networks* aiming to enable teachers to find their own solutions to the problems they face with their more difficult-to-teach pupils. The consultative case discussion model answers both these demands, in line with the warning that 'for pupils with emotional/behaviour problems, there are dangers in over-emphasis on "managing" the behaviour without attempts to understand the child's feelings' (National Curriculum Council, 1989b). It also recognises that children's behaviour sends us messages about their needs which we would lose if we merely wanted to 'manage' it (cf. Campbell, 1989; Laslett, 1989).

Warnings like these imply a move beyond a mainly *skills* perspective of in-service training to one addressed to extending perceptions and *understanding* of the problems in context. Most teachers have the skills; it is through lack of sufficient understanding, both of the children's needs and of what the display of such needs may do to them as teachers, that feelings and perceptions obstruct the deployment of their motivation and encouragement techniques – with the very children who need them most. Learning, on the other hand, through context-focused considerations, to see and respond appropriately to the underlying difficulties of a specific pupil will then not just have a beneficial effect on that pupil, but may indeed enhance the curriculum and learning opportunities for the whole class.

Thus, the case discussion model, with its problem-solving rather than ad hoc framework, is geared to sharpening teachers' recognition and deepening their understanding of children's needs in general while focusing on and exploring those of their neediest pupils, and enhancing teachers' abilities to meet these needs. It is designed to help them do so, *within the ordinary teaching day*; i.e., it does not suggest that teachers should take on the tasks of social workers or psychologists, but it alerts them to the so frequently untapped 'therapeutic' potential that exists in any teacher's educational repertoire.

How does the model achieve this? It taps this untapped potential, not by advising or 'telling' teachers how they might do their job differently – the more customary way of 'advising' which frequently mainly amounts to offering one's own solutions to another person's difficulty, but by using, in the context in which the difficulties are experienced, those *insight-generating interprofessional skills* which assist the participants in the exploration to find their *own* workable alternative solution.

I summarise what I have outlined in detail elsewhere (Hanko, 1986; 1987; 1989a, b; 1990); these are **the skills**:

- the skill of *asking answerable questions* (which may widen insights about a pupil's needs displayed in his or her behaviour, and how these needs might be responded to appropriately in the course of an ordinary teaching day, as an integral part of the professional task); asking such questions in a genuinely exploring, non-provocative, thus supportive way;
- the skill of *discovering*, from the answers to such questions, *the teacher's strengths and building on them*, and, through this sharing process, accepting and supplementing (rather than supplanting) any individual teacher's expertise with that of his or her colleagues and the supporting consultant's;
- the skill of *generating information that can help to highlight the issues* relating to the situation that is being explored in any one session.

And these are **the areas** on which one focuses the exploration, within which teachers' hidden, forgotten, unrealised skills may be elicited:

- *curriculum content and delivery* and how these may be adapted to the individual needs gauged in the exploration, as well as to those of the specific pupil's whole learning group;
- ordinary *classroom procedures* and the value signals that are sent out to pupils through the ways in which teachers and pupils relate, and in

which pupils among their peers are helped to relate to each other;
- *assessment patterns*: noting the extent to which they support, or threaten or diminish self-esteem;

in short, the very areas which the Elton Committee of Enquiry (DES, 1989) summarised as the differences between schools from comparable backgrounds, which influence the degree to which needs may remain unmet or even be created, with their consequences suffered by both pupils and teachers.

It is the supporter's task to help create the conditions conducive to such problem-exploration and to help produce a climate of commitment to do something about solving it. S/he will therefore avoid the traditional forms of giving advice, the kind of advice that can make teachers feel worse by implying that others can handle things better; that may seem to ignore the teacher's own expertise by trying to replace – rather than supplement – it; that offers one's own solutions to another person's problem (a notoriously ineffective way of solving problems); or colludes with expectations of 'expert advice' that reinforce the idea that children with such difficulties are qualitatively different, that their problem is 'out there', and that therefore only 'the experts' can deal with it.

Instead, this approach lets teachers experience the extent of their relevant expertise; taps their untapped or forgotten skills and develops these further; lets them *experience* that there is more common ground between children with more obvious difficulties and the majority of 'normal' children than that which seems to make them 'special', (so that what teachers offer specially to some will be seen to have relevance for others); and lets them *experience* how learning to respond more appropriately to one's most difficult-to-teach pupils can improve the quality of teaching and learning in the classroom and the school as a whole.

This in-service approach to support and training is thus concerned with staff development at several levels of the learning process: the cognitive (as information is generated that helps to highlight the underlying issues, and knowledge about the interactional aspects of children's special needs is supplemented); the perceptual/affective (as better understanding extends perception of the difficulty and influences reaction to it); and the interactional level. Here, the constant practice by staff in using their interprofessional skills training, both with children and, on their behalf, with often 'unhelpful' parents and fellow professionals, facilitates purposeful cooperation with the home and the institutional community as well as professionals from related services; while it enables teachers to decide for themselves on more appropriate alternative responses to the difficulty, having explored the problem and deepened their understanding of it.

As described in detail elsewhere (Hanko, 1990), this approach to staff development also addresses itself to the supporters' own support and training needs, the mismatch between the magnitude of their task and the minimal amount of training often offered; and the *in situ* training opportunities which it is possible to create through staff support sessions of their own, for developing their own interprofessional skills which may save them from being left 'stranded, resented and counter-productively (deemed to be) bearers of answers to problems which the school staff could be helped to resolve for themselves' (Sayer, 1987). We then assist them to extend their consultative role to school and classroom dynamics as well as to meeting the needs of individual children.

What all this amounts to is neither more nor less than a perspicacious redeployment of some of our child-related skills to working with fellow professionals, and an approach to staff development and support in which the staff, with some outside help, become a 'self-managing team', experiencing the benefits, for them and their pupils, that arise from a structured sharing of expertise and experience with others, both within and across institutions.

References

Adams, F. (1986) 'Teacher Support', *Education*, 7 March, p.218.
Bowman, I. (1986) 'Special Needs in Ordinary Classrooms', *European Journal of Special Education*, 1, p.137-8.
Campbell, D. (1989) 'A Psychoanalytic Contribution to Understanding Delinquents at School', *Journal of Educational Therapy*, 2, 4, pp.50-65.
Department of Education and Science (1989) *Discipline in Schools* (the Elton Report). London: HMSO.
Deveson, T. (1986) 'Learn to Understand', *Times Educational Supplement*, 14 Feb., p. 27.
Hanko, G. (1986) 'Social Workers as Teacher Consultants', *Journal of Social Work Practice*, 2, 2, pp. 88-106.
Hanko, G. (1987) 'Group Consultation with Mainstream Teachers', in Thacker, J. (Ed.), *Working with Groups*. DECP Monographs 3 and 4, pp. 123-30. Leicester: British Psychological Society.

Hanko, G. (1989a) 'Sharing Expertise: Developing the Consultative Role', in Evans, R. (Ed.) *Special Educational Needs: Policy and Practice*, pp. 67–80. Oxford: Blackwell.

Hanko, G. (1989b) 'After Elton – How to "Manage" Disruption?', *British Journal of Special Education*, **16**, 4, pp. 140–43.

Hanko, G. (1990) *Special Needs in Ordinary Classrooms – Supporting Teachers*. Second (enlarged) edn. Oxford: Blackwell. (First published 1985).

Laslett, R. (1989) 'Maladjusted Children's Learning', *Maladjustment and Therapeutic Education*, **7**, 3, pp. 186–8.

Mittler, P. (1990) 'Too difficult to address?', *Times Educational Supplement*, 23 Feb., p. 26.

Mongon, D. and Hart, S. (1989) *Improving Classroom Behaviour: New Directions for Teachers and Pupils*. London: Cassell.

National Curriculum Council (1989a) *Implementing the National Curriculum – Participation by Pupils with Special Educational Needs*. Circular Number 5. York: NCC.

National Curriculum Council (1989b) *Curriculum Guidance 2: A Curriculum for All*. York: NCC.

Sayer, J. (1987) *Secondary Schools for All? Strategies for Special Needs*. London: Cassell.

CHAPTER 9

Collaborative INSET and Special Educational Needs

Martyn Rouse and Maggie Balshaw

Introduction and background

This chapter provides details and preliminary evaluation of a joint Local Education Authority and higher education initiative designed to develop whole school approaches to meeting special educational needs. The focus of this chapter is on the rationale and historical context for the initiative, together with details of its structure and an analysis of the findings of a small scale evaluation project.

The in-service training courses which followed the implementation of the 1981 Education Act in Britain were the starting point for this initiative. Over recent years significant numbers of teachers have undertaken government funded one-term courses on special educational needs in the ordinary school (SENIOS). Eligible courses were defined as those which fell within one of four specified priority areas and which involved at least 20 days' attendance but lasting no longer than 12 months (Hegarty and Moses, 1988). A large number of such courses flourished and by 1984 Moses, Hegarty and Jowett (1987) were able to study 25 such courses, finding that they had four main characteristics: a taught element, a programme of school visits, information on various support services, and a school project or commission which was the key element in many of them.

These SENIOS courses had been successfully organised and run by the Cambridge Institute of Education (CIE) and the commission (school project) had been an important part. This commission was generally based in the school of the course member but the extent to which the project brought about change was unpredictable. Local investigations in Cambridgeshire and the research referred to above by Hegarty and Moses (1988) and that of Norwich and Cowne (1985) revealed a number of shortcomings in SENIOS courses. Briefly these were:

- there was no organised system of selection – it was 'hit and miss';
- there was no real preparation/negotiation in schools;
- there was no expectation of headteacher/rest of school involvement in any depth;
- the learning stopped with the teacher who 'did' the course. It was not effective in educating the school as a whole, as it dealt with skills rather than whole curriculum issues;
- there was no system of 'aftercare' and support to sustain any changes in attitudes and practice which might have occurred;
- the courses took no account of local and LEA need for school developments in responding to special needs.

More recently, government imposed changes in funding for In-Service Education for Teachers (INSET) have led to the belief that courses which involve the collaboration of schools, Local Education Authorities (LEAs) and higher education (HE) may well be central to INSET provision during the 1990s. Individual needs and local requirements will have to be met through courses which allow for the simultaneous development of professional expertise and whole school policies which arise from school development plans (Jeffs, 1987).

Recent trends in special needs and INSET

During the past decade there has been considerable development in thinking with regard to the concept of special educational needs. Briefly summarised these developments can be seen as a move from traditional thinking, i.e., special needs are within child, should be dealt with by 'experts', are categorised by handicapping and labelling conditions, should be dealt with separately through forms of segregation, and are static in nature, to more recent thinking which can be summarised in the following way: special needs are of an interactive or ecological nature, are to do with all teachers and whole schools, are seen as curricular needs, are characterised by normalisation and integration, and are of a dynamic nature. Figure 9.1 illustrates these points.

Figure 9.1   Special educational needs: the changing focus

Traditional	New
within child	interactive/ecological
experts	all teachers/whole schools
categories of	curricular needs
handicap/labels	
segregation/separation	integration/normalisation
static	dynamic

These changes in focus clearly must be reflected in the style and focus of INSET for special educational needs. In addition, widely documented in the literature is the development of advice about the nature of effective INSET. In response to these influences it is clear that INSET should move from taking a traditional disability perspective and move to an educational perspective. From a narrow curriculum focus it must move to a wide curriculum perspective, considering not just issues to do with testing for deficits in functioning, but encompassing classroom observation, assessment and recording. Another aspect involves shifting the focus of the course from the individual, to include both individual and institutional development. This involves seeing the course members as active participants who learn more from the process than they would if they were mere passive receivers. They participate in negotiating content rather than having it prescribed and engage as reflective practitioners who collaborate with their colleagues rather than becoming 'trained up' experts. These developments are illustrated in Figure 9.2.

Figure 9.2   Perspectives on INSET

Traditional	New
disability perspective	educational perspective
narrow curriculum focus	wide curriculum perspective
testing	observation, assessment and recording
individual development only	individual and institutional development
skills	process
passive receivers	active participants
content prescribed	content negotiated
'training up' experts	developing staff collaboration and reflective practitioners

Underpinning the establishment of the new initiative were eight principles which broadly reflected the aspects detailed above of both changing trends in the concept of special educational needs and the forms of INSET most appropriate to these changes. The new initiative was clearly perceived to have three major phases in an attempt to avoid some of the shortcomings detailed earlier and in order to incorporate some of the perceived wisdom with regard to effective staff development to be found in the literature: Powers (1983), Fullan (1982), Joyce and Showers (1988), Hopkins (1989), and Loucks-Horsley *et al.* (1987).

The eight principles

Phase 1

(1) *Local knowledge and collaboration* amongst all participants are positive pre-requisites to an INSET initiative such as this.
(2) *Negotiation* should be carried out to try and ensure that school and individual needs are met.
(3) *LEA involvement and support* is to be seen as an integral part in order to meet LEA, area, local and school needs.
(4) *The course aims and ethos* need to take into account the current position on thinking and practice in meeting special educational needs, and the aims should be differentiated to meet a variety of needs.

Phase 2

(5) *The structure* should allow preparation, negotiation, needs identification, practice and feedback, and support.
(6) *Whole school approaches* should be integral to the school-based development so all personnel are involved at the appropriate level.

Phase 3

(7) *'Ownership'* by the school of the work should be encouraged at an early stage to enhance the chances of maintaining initiatives in the follow-up phase, where 'ownership' or 'institutionalisation' can be seen as criteria for successful change (this is important throughout all three phases).
(8) *Long-term review and support* should be built in from the early stages and maintained for a considerable period in phase 3. INSET without 'aftercare' is seen as very vulnerable, so an attempt to ensure continuing development and change should exist as central to the course re-design.

The course

The establishment of this new initiative in 1986 came about as a result of discussions between LEA advisory personnel and tutorial staff at CIE. Taking the principles outlined previously it was hoped that in focusing on a small geographical area and employing these, there would be benefits for pupils, schools and the LEA which had not been evident in the old modes of course delivery. By focusing upon this local area, initial involvement, support throughout and continued aftercare by the LEA advisory team, based in the special needs resource centre, would be easier to organise.

The course team

A course team normally consists of five people: two LEA area coordinators for special educational needs (advisers), two external support teachers who have direct involvement with the schools selected for the course, and a tutor from CIE. An important feature of this initiative is the joint involvement of LEA personnel in planning, delivery and evaluation. To improve communication and commitment particular geographical areas are targeted each year. It is the support teachers for these localities who then join the course team.

This arrangement facilitates the availability of information and support throughout all three phases of a course. The course is then available in different parts of the LEA in subsequent years. Consequently there is continuity in the course team in that the tutor from CIE and the two members of the LEA advisory team do not change, whilst the two support teachers are new each year and bring fresh perspectives and detailed information about their schools. This structure provides the LEA support teachers with the chance of working on a substantial INSET course under supervision and gives them numerous opportunities to consider and develop their own skills as providers of staff development (Miles, Saxl and Lieberman, 1988; Davies and Davies, 1988).

Stages

There are three discernible stages to the initiative, in line with the principles outlined previously:

– *Phase 1*, the pre-course phase during which schools are invited by the LEA to review their existing policies and practice for meeting special educational need with a view to agreeing on an area for development. Although no specific process is suggested, it is hoped that schools would go through a GRIDS-type exercise (McMahon *et al.*, 1984) in order to select the topic for development within the school. This topic forms the basis of the school based project. In recent years schools have been encouraged to link the project to their school development plan, and National Curriculum initiatives.

In order to explain to schools the aims of the course and the nature and purpose of the policy review, headteachers and interested members of teaching staff are invited to local meetings which are addressed by the course coordinator from CIE and representatives of the LEA. This informal forum provides the opportunity for clarifying issues and answering points of concern. At the meeting it is stressed that this initiative is not merely a course for the individual to attend but is designed to enable school development to occur. Indeed, it is the school which is coming on the course and the headteacher and staff select a course member who acts as the school's 'delegate'.

After carrying out their review, schools are invited to make a submission outlining details of their proposed topic for development. An important element of this phase could therefore be seen as being contractual. The submissions are considered by the CIE tutor and the LEA support staff and any necessary amendments are discussed. Not all submissions are accepted, particularly those in which it is clear that insufficient consultations with the staff of the school have taken place.

During Phase 1, a day conference for course participants and their headteacher is arranged at the CIE during which there is negotiation about course content. The opportunity is also taken to remind participating schools about their commitment to supporting the course member.

– *Phase 2* covers the taught part of the course when participants attend the CIE on Fridays over two terms plus a full week block in each term (23 days in all). During this phase, course participants are expected to develop, with their colleagues, a response to the project topic. This takes the form of action planning within the overall planned development. At the end of this phase participants produce a written account of their project. This phase is described in more detail later in the chapter.

– *Phase 3* is the post-course phase during which the LEA is committed to providing support for course members and their schools to enable the project to become institutionalised. A follow-up day conference takes place about nine months after the end of the taught part of the course. There are two aims for this day. One concerns accountability – how is the project going? What has been achieved? The second purpose is to provide participants with the opportunity to share successful strategies with each other. It is interesting to note that participants from early cohorts continue to meet on a regular basis as self supporting groups.

Professional developments for participants

Whilst the focus of this initiative is on school development, it is strongly felt that course members should benefit personally. It is necessary to point out that course members are all experienced teachers. Most of them carry the responsibility for coordinating their school's response to special educational needs. As Miles and Huberman (1983) point out, motives such as professional development and career opportunities are at least as important as the content of innovation and its possibilities for helping pupils. With this in mind credits towards the Institute's Modular Advanced Diploma in Educational Studies are awarded to those students who wish to continue to work towards further qualifications.

Course content and methods of study

This is not the place to go into detail about the course content but whilst there are areas of knowledge such as legislation, the implications of disability, local support services and curriculum issues to be covered, the balance of the course is moving towards greater emphasis on understanding schools as organisations, working effectively with colleagues and winning friends and influencing people. The course attempts to:

- be owned by, and relevant to, the participants
- be interactive in style
- make learning active, experiential and fun
- ensure the school-based project provides positive action for the future
- equip participants with the skills to effect and evaluate that action
- be of benefit to pupils by facilitating teacher and school development.

Evaluating the initiative

After three years of this initiative the present authors felt that a formal evaluation should be carried out to assess the effectiveness of the initiative. This was seen as additional to the formative and summative evaluation carried out in collaboration with each cohort of course members, during and at the end of Phase 2 (the actual course). Criteria for this formal evaluation would be the ways in which schools had been dealing with special needs issues, and how changes in attitudes and practice had been facilitated and supported.

In this chapter it is not possible to give full details of the research methods used to investigate the initiative; these are documented in Balshaw (1990). In brief, a combination of postal survey of the three first cohorts followed by a series of interviews with headteachers, course participants and LEA support team members, were carried out.

The evaluation of staff development programmes designed to bring about change in schools is acknowledged to be complex because of the large number of variables involved. Joyce and Showers (1988) refer to variables which are interlinked and need to be considered in this way when evaluating an INSET initiative. These variables are the teachers, the institutions, the training programme and also the students or pupils. Evidence was found that in each of these sets of variables, change had occurred as a result of the initiative. Briefly, there was evidence that change had occurred:

for individual teachers in:
- their confidence and self-esteem
- their skills and self appraisal
- their ability to be open with colleagues

for schools in:
- INSET and staff development which improved teachers' skills
- INSET and staff development leading to changes in classroom practice
- the development of new 'norms' and ethos
- the types and range of support received

for pupils in:
- curriculum provision
- types and range of support received.

There was evidence that certain aspects of course design and delivery need more careful attention. These are:

- making best possible use of local knowledge in reviewing the needs of schools
- making the submissions resulting from these negotiations assume the level of contractual commitment from all sides
- ensuring that all the local special needs centre staff team are involved as much as possible to guard against discontinuity through support staff changes
- making the best use of the initial day conference to determine the participants' needs and negotiate the content
- making sure that the best possible use is made of the time the head and course member spend together on the course
- attempting to build in a more reliable system of 'aftercare' at both formal and informal levels.

Three other issues have arisen from the evaluation of this initiative. The first concerns staff changes. Some schools found that change of staff, other than the course member, was a positive rather than a negative factor. However, there were comments about changes in the local special needs centre staff having negative outcomes. Such changes seriously impair attempts to provide continued support and aftercare.

The second point concerns the difficulty many teachers (both course members and their colleagues in school) had in identifying positive outcomes for pupils. They were not suggesting that there were no outcomes for pupils, but such benefits were explained as changes in teachers' behaviour such as greater confidence, more positive attitudes and curricular and organisational change. They argued that this would lead to benefit for pupils.

The third issue concerns the importance of the headteacher's support. This was seen as the most crucial factor by most teachers interviewed. Without the active support of the head, progress was extremely slow when compared with schools where the head gave personal, organisational and practical support.

Conclusion

The experience of the teachers who have been involved in this initiative, and their colleagues back in school, seems to have been, in the main, positive. They appear to have experienced some of the attributes of effective teacher development programmes, and the comments made by participants, both on the course, and in the school projects, certainly seem to reflect those made in the literature. As Loucks-Horsley *et al.* (1987) say:

> Staff development experiences that build on collegiality, collaboration, discovery and solving real problems of teaching and learning summon the strength within a staff instead of just challenging them to measure up to somebody else's standard. The focal point for staff development is the individual working with others, trying to do the best possible job of educating children.

This positive staff development experience seems to have facilitated the change processes in the schools. It has enabled involvement in the projects to lead towards ownership of the changes. As Fullan (1982) advises, this involvement is a crucial factor in managing the process of change:

> Conceptual clarity ... cannot be achieved at the outset through specific goal statements, lectures and packaged materials; it must be accomplished during implementation as people try things and discuss them. And it is important for understanding and consolidating the change in practice.

The collaborative nature of the way in which the teachers on the course had worked together helped them to work in conjunction with their colleagues back in school. This seems to have instilled, through the model of practice and feedback, a confidence which leads to competence. As one participant described it, this collaborative approach had worked well in her situation.

> I think that a course that involves a member of staff coming back and working closely with other members of staff is a very good one. That to me is an ideal way of getting changes in schools ... actually getting people involved in what you are doing and then getting feedback.

This observation is echoed in the advice of Joyce and Showers (1988) in describing effective staff development.

> Effective staff development requires cooperative relationships that break down the isolation and increase the collective strength of the community of educators who staff the school.

In conclusion, we offer a set of conditions which would seem to be necessary for the success of such a venture:

- initial negotiation involving all staff of the school to identify development needs

- formulating a contract between the individual, the school, the LEA and higher education
- a taught element which stresses process as well as content
- interactive presentation
- projects which are likely to be of benefit to pupils
- active support of the headteacher
- opportunities for course members to pursue their own professional development and career opportunities
- formative evaluation across the whole programme and summative evaluation of the project as well as the course
- continued post-course support for participants and their schools.

A failure to take note of some or all of these factors could well result in the waste of valuable time, effort and resources, and a less effective system of INSET for special educational needs in ordinary schools.

It is also hoped that the radical changes which are in the process of restructuring the education service in England and Wales will allow sufficient funding to enable such initiatives to continue and to seek ways of improving schools through collaborative INSET.

References

Balshaw, M. (1990) 'INSET and the Change Process in Schools'. Unpublished MA assignment, CIE.

Davies, J. and Davies, P. (1988) 'Developing Credibility as a Support and Advisory Teacher', *Support for Learning* 3, 1, pp. 12–15.

Fullan, M. (1982) *The Meaning of Educational Change*. New York: Teachers' College Press.

Hegarty, S. and Moses, D. (1988) *Developing Expertise*. Windsor: NFER-Nelson.

Hopkins, D. (1989) *Evaluation for School Development*. Milton Keynes: Open University Press.

Huberman, A. and Miles, M. (1983) *Innovation Up Close: A Field Study in Twelve School Outings*. Andover, MA: The Network Inc.

Jeffs, A. (1987) 'SENIOS–INSET Sense in Action', *Inspection and Advice*, 22, 2, pp. 19–22.

Joyce, B. and Showers, B. (1988) *Student Achievement through Staff Development*. New York: Longman.

Loucks-Horsley, S. *et al.* (1987) *Continuing to Learn*. Andover, MA: The Network Inc.

McMahon, A., Bolam, R., Abbott, R. and Holly, P. (1984) *Guidelines for Review and Development in Schools (GRIDS) Primary Handbook*. York: Longman/Schools Council.

Miles, M., Saxl, E. and Lieberman, A. (1988) 'What Skills do Educational "Change Agents" Need? An Empirical View', *Curriculum Inquiry* 18, 2, pp. 157–93.

Moses, D., Hegarty, S. and Jowett, S. (1987) 'Meeting Special Educational Needs. Support for the Ordinary School', *Educational Research*, **29**, 2, pp. 108–15.

Norwich, B. and Cowne, E. (1985) 'Training with a School Focus', *British Journal of Special Education*, **12**, 4, pp. 167–70.

Powers, D.A. (1983) 'Mainstreaming and the In-service Education of Teachers', *Exceptional Children*, **49**, 5, pp. 432–9.

CHAPTER 10

Collaboration in Initial Training

Rachel David and Beryl Smith

Over a period of five years the present authors have been involved in overseeing a shared training project involving student teachers and student speech therapists. The former were on an initial teacher-training course in severe learning difficulties at Westhill College, Birmingham, UK. This course prepared students for teaching in both special and ordinary schools. The student speech therapists were on a course in speech and language pathology and therapeutics at the City of Birmingham Polytechnic. Both sets of students were in the third year of four-year honours degree courses at the time the project took place.

Staff in the two institutions were of the opinion that although students accepted the idea of collaboration between professions and received input from a variety of professionals involved in the education of children with learning difficulties, they needed the opportunity to put collaboration into practice and to reflect upon its principles. A full account of the two training institutions and an evaluation of the project at the end of the first year appears in David and Smith (1987).

For the purpose of the project a simple definition of collaboration was used – working together for the good of the client. In an attempt to identify and promote the principles of collaboration we continued to evaluate and modify the framework of the project over the five year period. It became apparent that 'working together' could benefit not only the child but also the professionals involved, be they the students or the staff who masterminded the scheme. During the lifespan of the

102

project there have been many reports of collaboration in the field of special educational needs. These include collaboration between teachers of children with hearing impairment and speech therapists (Whitehouse *et al.*, 1987) collaboration between professionals and parents (Wolfendale, 1988) between teachers and pupils (Gersch, 1987) between pupil and pupil (Topping, 1987). The principles of collaboration are of importance across these various situations.

Outline of the project

The aims of the project remained valid throughout. They were:

(1)   To improve communication between teachers and speech therapists and to increase their understanding of one another's contribution to the management of speech and language problems in young children.
(2)   To enable students to become familiar with some of the assessment techniques used by the two disciplines.
(3)   To encourage teamwork and production of realistic and relevant remedial programmes which can be carried out in a school setting.

These aims encompassed several factors which were considered of importance in promoting collaboration, including knowledge of each others' special skills, effective communication and involvement in a joint enterprise.

Accordingly, pairs of students, (teachers and speech therapists) jointly observed, assessed and wrote reports on a young child with speech and language problems. The children were situated in a variety of settings, including special schools, day centres, nurseries and special units. Emphasis was placed upon the requirement that the report should contain realistic and relevant suggestions for remediation programmes which could be carried out by teachers as part of their daily routine in the classroom or unit.

Changes to the framework of the project

Over the five years, feedback from students contributed to modifications in the preparation given and the pattern of student involvement. More time, for instance, was allowed for teachers to gain familiarity with the assessment tools used by speech therapists, although the latter were urged to make use of observational techniques in this situation, rather than rely heavily on standardised tests. From the second year onwards each pair of students met before going into school in order to discuss an outline plan of action, but after the teacher had observed the child in school on a previous occasion. In this way it was hoped to simulate the real-life situation in which the teacher has prior knowledge of the child in her class. From the third year onwards, students were given an outline of the Whitehouse *et al.* (1987) model and an opportunity to discuss during the preparatory session.

Greater emphasis was placed on the production of 'realistic and relevant' remediation programmes and these were made available to the school. This meant that programmes had not only to be appropriate to the child's speech or language needs but were also required to identify particularly important aspects for remedial work, rather than the whole range of needs. Suggested activities should be of interest to the child, the teacher and possibly to other children in the class. They should be easily incorporated into everyday class activities and be capable of being evaluated and developed further, according to response.

Evaluation

Evaluation carried out by questionnaire at the completion of each year's exercise revealed that with few exceptions the students enjoyed the project and rated it useful or very useful. All wanted to carry on with such collaboration in the future. Typical comments included:

> It provided the opportunity to work in equal partnership with another trainee professional. We were shown both sides of points of view.

> It built up my confidence for working with other professionals.

Participants were of the opinion that collaborative teamwork could provide a better product than individual working because

(a) It facilitates a balanced assessment of the whole child. Whilst teachers are skilled in the use of observational techniques and criterion-referenced assessment and are able to observe a child in a range of classroom situations over a period of time, speech therapists have the additional resources to provide a more detailed analysis of the child's speech and language in relation to other aspects of development.

(b) Teachers will be more motivated to participate in remediation activities if they have also contributed to the assessment process. A situation in which the speech therapist takes the main responsibility for assessment and subsequently offers advice to the teacher, could be less motivating for the teacher than one in which both work as equals, sharing information and resources.

(c) Intervention is likely to be more realistic and appropriate as a result of collaboration between the two professions. The individual contributions of the teacher and the therapist will combine to give a deeper and broader view of the child's development and difficulties. The teacher's greater familiarity with the child and his or her interests complements the speech therapist's more specialised understanding of the child's communication. A speech therapist who is aware of the aims and methods of the teacher will be better able to suggest appropriate ways of helping the child, whilst the teacher will gain an increased understanding of the child's problems and of the aims and techniques of the speech therapist.

(d) The advantages of team-work extend beyond the individual child. The teacher will acquire skills for encouraging language development and identifying children with language difficulties which will be of use with a wider group of children. The speech therapist will learn about the demands of the curriculum and classroom routine. Both professions will gain an increased understanding of child development and a greater ability to manage children with speech and language difficulties in the educational setting.

Factors which facilitated collaboration in this project

Students were asked to suggest factors which facilitate collaboration. Their opinions were impressively insightful. Some of the factors mentioned were:

    understanding what each has to offer

    respect for each other's expertise

    a positive attitude to teamwork and collaboration, not competition

    having an honest approach and attempting to share knowledge, not adopting an 'expert' role

    enough time for joint consultations

    being prepared to listen and discuss

    developing a relationship of trust

From the evidence of the evaluation it appears that factors increasing the likelihood of successful interprofessional collaboration fall into three main categories. These are, first, a willingness to abandon preconceptions about another's role. Second, an ability and willingness to share one's own knowledge and skills. Third, an ability to disregard personal professional status where there are discrepancies.

Factors which can militate against successful collaboration

Students made fewer comments on these but evidence may be derived from personal experience and the literature. Despite support among professionals working in the field for the principle of collaboration, there are circumstances which create difficulties or may preclude any attempt at successful collaboration.

An influential factor with respect to joint working between teachers and speech therapists may be a lack of encouragement at managerial level. The partners are employed by different agencies (Education and Health Services). The two may not relate at management/policy-making level. As Wedell (1987) points out 'Effective collaboration between members of different professions can and does occur through the goodwill and inspiration of individuals within the services. However, if it is to be assured, collaboration must actually be seen as a substantive objective of those responsible for the services'. Lack of previous experience of successful partnership may also deter participants and the importance of experience at the training stage is also emphasised by Wedell (1987). Other factors include lack of time for consultation, often exacerbated by different working patterns. The speech therapist may provide a visiting service only. Staff changes may also disrupt working relationships. With regard to these, the need for a stable system is highlighted, into which new staff can slot. Lack of physical accommodation may cause difficulties in some instances as may personality clashes or ideological differences. Collaboration cannot be forced upon professionals but it can be encouraged and the path smoothed if both facilitating and inhibiting factors are recognised. Management support is essential.

The need for a model

We learned from the paired student project that a model of practice, developed and agreed between the participants is desirable.

Within the time constraints of the project it was not possible for the students to administer the remedial programmes, re-assess the child's needs and continue the collaboration. A far more complete model of practice has been developed as the result of partnership between speech therapists and teachers involved with hearing impaired children (see Figure 10.1, from Whitehouse *et al.*, 1987).

The first four stages of the Whitehouse *et al.* (1987) model sum up the steps in our paired student project. The further phases are essential for an effective outcome of the collaboration and take it beyond the

Figure 10.1   Proposed model of phases in the development of a partnership between speech therapists and teachers of the deaf (Whitehouse *et al.*, 1987)

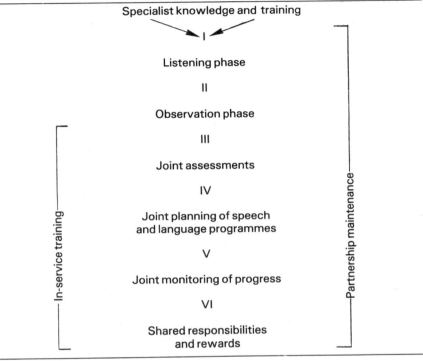

Specialist knowledge and training

I

Listening phase

II

Observation phase

III

Joint assessments

IV

Joint planning of speech
and language programmes

V

Joint monitoring of progress

VI

Shared responsibilities
and rewards

In-service training

Partnership maintenance

assessment stage and into joint remedial work. Joint monitoring of progress follows naturally from joint assessment. Sharing of responsibility for the child's management continues to be essential if the process of intervention is to be appropriate to his or her educational or communicative needs.

Maintenance of professional collaboration requires repeated consolidation of all the phases specified in the model. Thus the participants must continue to discuss information relating to their own professional viewpoints as well as to the children with whom they are concerned. Both formal and informal meetings may take place. Observation of each other's work is to be encouraged and joint assessment, evaluation and planning should also continue.

Whitehouse *et al.* (1987) place particular emphasis on the role of in-service training in partnership maintenance. It is important that each participant provides training for the other in areas of their own expertise. In addition, training for both participants in areas of shared interest should facilitate shared working.

108

For effective management of the partnership, it may be advisable for participants to draw up clear contracts relating to each one's responsibilities and to allot adequate time for joint planning, assessment, monitoring and evaluation, with agreement on timetables for regular meetings.

Conclusions

The principles of collaboration explored here can be applied over a broad spectrum of situations in which 'partnership' is a desired outcome. The movement towards working together in the field of special education, which has repercussions for professionals, parents, carers, clients and pupils alike, is not one which is isolated from practice in mainstream. It is the result of a wider acceptance that involvement of participants is an important aim in any undertaking if maximum effectiveness is to be achieved in terms of outcome. This philosophy has been given impetus by changes in political and social beliefs and is supported by psychological research into learning and doing.

The findings from this shared project indicate that where initial effort and time is invested in establishing collaborative working patterns and subsequently in their maintenance, rewards will be reaped by professionals in terms of increased understanding of each other's aims and techniques and also of the nature and implications of the child's difficulties. However, perhaps no better reason for pursuing the concept of collaboration can be found than that given by Nieuwenhuis (1990) when describing a team approach to head injury. The conclusion was that such an approach provided the child involved and her family with a coordinated service. Most importantly, from the point of view of the present writers, it ' ... placed them [the child and her family] at the centre of our activities focusing on their needs rather than on our individual professional roles'.

References

David, R. and Smith, B. (1987) 'Preparing for Collaborative Working', *British Journal of Special Education*, **14**, 1, pp. 19–23.
Gersch, I. (1987) 'Involving Pupils in their own Assessment', in Bowers, A. (Ed.) *Special Educational Needs and Human Resource Management*. London: Croom Helm.
Nieuwenhuis, R. (1990) 'A Team Approach to Head Injury', *Therapy Weekly*, Jan. 18, p. 7.

Topping, K.J. (1987) *The Peer Tutoring Handbook: Promoting Cooperative Learning*. London: Croom Helm.

Wedell, K. (1987) 'The Integration and Meeting of Children's Special Educational Needs', *Proceedings of the Ninth National Conference, College of Speech Therapists*, **1**, pp. 9–16.

Whitehouse, J., Beazley, S. and Jones, H. (1987) 'Establishing Partnerships between Speech Therapists and Teachers involved with Hearing-impaired Children', *Proceedings of the Ninth National Conference, College of Speech Therapists*, **1**, pp. 189–207.

Wolfendale, S. (1988) *The Parental Contribution to Assessment*. Stratford upon Avon: NCSE.

CHAPTER 11

Consultative-collaborative Resource Teaching as a Means of Improving Special Education Service Delivery

D. Richard Freeze and Winston Rampaul

How special educators help children in need continues to change (e.g., Ainscow, 1990; Gartner and Lipsky, 1987; Stainback and Stainback, 1985; Wiesinger, 1986).

Psychometric measures once used to label children for the purposes of placement, funding, and to provide a pseudo-medical diagnosis of each child have given way to measures whch are ecological, data-based, curriculum-based, and intended to improve and guide future instruction and classroom management. Special educators have shifted their focus from 'What's wrong with the child?' to 'How can we educate the child better?'.

Models of direct service to special needs students in segregated settings by special education teachers (e.g., Deno, 1970) are being replaced by models of indirect service where the special educator acts as a support to the teacher and child in the regular classroom (e.g., Wang, 1980). Special education is no longer a preserve of experts supplying a special service to selected children; instead, it is becoming a way to provide the best possible education for all children. It has become an integral part of the evolution of an equitable, egalitarian, non-exclusionary, and professionally developed educational system.

The Consultative-collaborative (CC) model (see Bravi, 1988; Freeze, Bravi and Rampaul, 1989) exemplifies one way that data-based and curriculum-based assessment methods have been successfully integrated into a comprehensive indirect special education service

110

delivery approach. A series of research studies on the effectiveness of the model in a Canadian school division report positive effects for students and high levels of support for the model from special educators, classroom teachers, school administrators, instructional assistants, clinicians, and parents (see Bravi and Freeze, 1987a, 1987b; Freeze, 1988; Freeze and Bravi, 1987a, 1987b, 1987c, 1988).

Consultative-collaborative Model

In order to set the stage for a discussion of assessment methods in the context of this form of indirect service delivery, the key characteristics of the CC model are outlined.

Non-categorical approach. The idea that a child can be defined by his or her impairment, disability, or low achievement is rejected in the CC model. It is the whole child, with all of his or her interests, abilities, feelings, skills, ideas, and aspirations, who may be one focus of our attention. However, it is the child *in situ* that is of real importance. This means that all of the variables in the teaching–learning context must be considered in a holistic fashion. Such factors include: (a) the classroom climate and physical environment, (b) the teacher's methods of instruction, motivation, and behavior management, (c) the appropriateness of the curriculum to the students' needs, (d) the effectiveness of instructional materials, (e) the usefulness of evaluative methods in providing corrective feedback to students and identifying priorities for future instruction to the teacher, (f) the attitudes and interests of teachers and students, (g) the support services available in the classroom, and (h) the societal and familial contexts of schooling.

While impairments, disabilities, developmental differences, and the quality of past instruction and achievement do need to be taken into consideration; neither the student nor the teacher need be blamed in the CC model. The problem is perceived as a mismatch between what is being taught and what needs to be learned and may have more to do with the classroom ecology, curriculum content, teaching strategies, or instructional materials than with either the student or teacher. In an important sense, it is the pedagogical characteristics of the regular classroom that are the target of every special education intervention.

Indirect service bias. The primary purpose of the special educator in the CC model is to provide support to the classroom teacher working in the regular classroom. In order to prevent the use of exclusionary or deviant-status placements as routine strategies, the assumption is always made that the environment where the child belongs is the regular classroom. Only when all possibilities for success in the regular classroom have been exhausted and when success in an alternative setting can be predicted from data-based and curriculum-based measures, is the student placed away from the regular classroom. In the CC model, alternative placements have no permanent enrollment and no purposes independent of eventual re-entry into the regular classroom. They are temporary, usually part-time, and always involve on-going consultations and collaborative teaching between the special educator and the classroom teacher.

This does not mean, however, that special educators never work with children in one-to-one or small group formats. As examples, specialist teachers may work with children outside classrooms to (a) administer curriculum-based academic interviews or tests, (b) try out novel teaching methods prior to their introduction into the classroom, (c) teach academic skills or behavioral routines required for success in the classroom, or to (d) extend the curriculum in order to meet unique needs (such as speech and language services for students with communication disorders, mobility training for visually impaired students, personal and community living skills for mentally handicapped students, etc.). In addition, special educators may also work to serve individuals and small groups inside the classroom. As examples, they may work in the classroom to (a) conduct data-based behavioral observations, (b) implement early identification screening procedures, (c) demonstrate new teaching methods, (d) help differentiate classroom instruction, or (e) establish cooperative learning groups.

In all cases, the specialist teacher's involvement is part-time, short-term, and designed to support and enhance teaching and learning in the regular classroom for all students.

Professional development. The indirect service approach adopted in the CC model allows special educators and ordinary teachers to join forces in the prevention of future teaching–learning problems. A consultation or collaboration with a special educator that introduces the classroom teacher to more effective methods may have a positive impact on many other students in the future. Additionally, the special education teacher who visits classrooms throughout the school and who works with teachers at all grade levels and in all subjects areas is strategically placed to note broad patterns of success and difficulty. Such observations may lead to recommendations to school administrators with respect to: (a) successful teaching and behavior management practices, (b) peer coaching opportunities among teachers, (c) staff professional development needs, and (d) possible foci for curricular, programmatic, or administrative reviews.

Levels of service delivery and professional roles. The CC model involves six levels of service delivery. The first level is provided by the classroom teacher, possibly in conjunction with teaching assistants, volunteers, or in a cooperative teaching relationship with one or more other teachers.

The second level refers to teams of teachers. The teacher team is the initial form of assistance available to the classroom teacher. They may be organized around year levels (e.g., primary years teachers, senior forms teachers, etc.), subject areas (e.g., English literature, mathematics, etc.), special interests (e.g., whole language instruction, environmental sciences, etc.), or school programs (e.g., vocational program, performing arts, etc.).

The resource teacher is at the third level of service delivery. The resource teacher is a certified school-based special educator with previous regular classroom teaching experience and a full year of post-baccalaureate university training in special education. The resource teacher plays the pivotal role in special education service delivery in the CC model.

The in-school support services team is at the fourth level of service delivery. The in-school support team is constructed on a case-by-case basis when other levels of service delivery are in need of additional assistance. Team personnel might include a school administrator, a counsellor, the resource teacher, classroom teachers, a relevant clinical specialist, parents, students – anyone who might assist in problem solving. The 'case' need not be a specific child, it may be a general program designed to meet the needs of several teachers and many students. For example, early screening, peer tutoring, home reading, writing conferencing, computer-assisted instruction, and many other generic programs may be set up through the work of in-school support teams.

At the fifth and sixth levels of service delivery are services supplied through the school division's head office and ancillary services based in the community outside the school system. It is the resource teacher's responsibility to apply for extra-school services when necessary.

Service delivery phases. The CC model is divided into five operational phases of service delivery which are illustrated in Figure 11.1.

The Assistance Request Phase is usually initiated by the classroom teacher, although students, parents, teacher's assistants, administrators, or clinicians also may do so. The teacher's request may be

Figure 11.1 Operational phases and decision-making in the Consultative-collaborative Model of special education service delivery

Phase/ Duration	Resource Teacher Activities	Consultation and Collaboration with the Classroom Teacher
Assistance request (1–5 days)	• Review assistance request form • Review student file • Review grade level curriculum • Contact significant people (parents, previous teachers, specialists, etc.) • Schedule assistance request conference with teacher	• Clarify roles • Specify reasons for assistance request • Explore possible behavioral and instructional objectives • Schedule in-class observation • Schedule curriculum-based assessment procedures • Arrange home contact
Assessment (5–10 days)	• In-class observations • Academic interviews • Work sample analysis • Curriculum-based testing • Ecological assessment • Curriculum analysis • Analytic teaching • Develop 'diagnostic analysis'	• Review 'diagnostic analysis' • Set instructional and behavioral objectives • Determine measurement systems • Set criteria for success for all objectives in the measurement systems • Explore behavior management and instructional methods • Consider referral to another level of service delivery
Program Development (1–10 days)	• Develop instructional methods and materials • Develop behavior management and/or motivational strategy • Develop measurement checklists, charts, graphs, etc. • Designate personnel and other resources • Trial teaching • Outline liaison with other support services if needed	• Review instructional methods and materials • Review behavior management and/or motivational strategy • Review measurement system • Agree on resource utilization and personnel responsibilities • Schedule sequence of instruction in program implementation • Verify criteria for success and specify target mastery dates • Arrange home contact
Program Implementation (1–8 weeks)	• Demonstration teaching • Team teaching in classroom • Short-term, part-time alternative placement • Support for differentiated instruction in the classroom	• On-going consultation between Resource and Classroom Teachers • Continuous direct measurement of instruction • Continuous direct measurement of behavior • Monitoring of sequence of instruction and achievement of criteria for success

		• Transfer alternative program to classroom if necessary • Fine tune program and program supports in the classroom • Maintain home contact
Case Closure (Variable)	• Evaluate mastery against target dates and criteria for success • Evaluate if program is 'up and running' toward mastery target dates and success criteria independently in classroom	• Close case if criteria for success have been met • Re-enter assessment phase if criteria for success are not being met by target dates • Consider referral to another level of service delivery • Agree on probes for monitoring maintenance and/or generalization of program gains to be implemented by classroom teacher • Conclude home contact

Note: Adapted from Freeze, Bravi and Rampaul (1989).

concerned with a particular student, a group of students, a general behavior management problem, or teaching–learning mismatch in the classroom. As illustrated in Figure 11.1, the resource teacher collects existing information about the assistance request and meets the classroom teacher to set the CC process in motion.

The purpose of the Assessment Phase is to collect and analyze data-based and curriculum-based information to guide future instruction. Data-based information is collected through in-class observations using a continuous chronologue as well as behavior sampling methods such as event recording, duration recording, time sampling, or latency recording (see Bachor and Crealock, 1986; Kerr and Nelson, 1983). Curriculum-based information is collected through (a) the analysis of student work samples drawn from sources such as student workbooks, teacher-made tests, or student assignments (see Zigmond, Vallecorsa and Silverman, 1983), (b) academic interviews (see Freeze, 1990), (c) curriculum-based testing (see Howell and Morehead, 1987; Mercer and Mercer, 1985), (d) analysis of the curriculum including prerequisite knowledge, level of materials, recommended teaching strategies, motivational techniques, and evaluative procedures (see Kameenui and Simmons, 1990), (e) sociometric and ecological assessments of the classroom (see Bachor and Crealock, 1986), (f) criterion-referenced probes to estimate students' skills (White and

Haring, 1980), (g) assessments of students' prior knowledge (e.g., the Pre-reading Plan developed by Langer, 1981), and (h) analytic teaching through which different instructional approaches are tried in mini-lessons and analyzed for effectiveness. The results of the assessment are synthesized in a diagnostic analysis which is used as a basis for program development in conjunction with the classroom teacher.

The Program Development Phase is based on the decisions which have emerged from consultations between the classroom and resource teachers. The purpose of program development is to plan for differentiated classroom instruction so that all students' needs are met.

The goal of the Program Implementation Phase is to get an appropriate program 'up and running' in the classroom. To this end the resource teacher may (a) coach the classroom teacher, (b) demonstrate new methods in the classroom, or (c) team teach with the classroom teacher in a mutually planned approach. In some instances, the resource teacher may work with one or more students in an alternative setting on a short term basis to achieve specific objectives designed to maximize the chances of classroom success in the context of the new program. In instances where generic programs are being introduced into one or more classrooms, the resource teacher may collaborate with several teachers and classroom groups.

The Case Closure Phase is designed to bring an end to the process based on pre-set criteria. If the criteria for success have not been met, then consideration must be given to re-entering the process at an earlier phase of the model and to seeking assistance at another level of service delivery.

Home-school partnership. When a particular student is involved, the classroom teacher stays in communication with a home contact throughout the phases of the CC model. In some cases, parents are invited to consultations between the classroom and resources teachers. In all cases, parents participate in decision-making that affects student placement or involves the in-school or divisional support services teams. As a general rule of thumb, parents are involved as soon as their child is to be treated differently from the other students in his or her class. Parents prefer to be informed about school programs that affect their children (Freeze, 1988; Freeze and Bravi, 1987c). In addition, informed parents are more willing to work actively with school personnel.

Merger of 'special' and 'regular' education. The CC model is an actualization of the idea of merging special and regular education (see

Gartner and Lipsky, 1987: Stainback and Stainback, 1985). The foundations of this merging are the data-based and curriculum-based measures that ensure that special educators remain on target in terms of what is happening in the regular classroom.

Assessment for instruction

Data-based and curriculum-based measures can be used for a variety of purposes including pre-testing, formative and summative evaluations, and diagnostic assessment. In the context of the CC model, the emphasis is placed on diagnostic assessment to guide instruction.

Diagnostic analysis

Information collected during the Assistance Request and Assessment phases is synthesized in a diagnostic analysis. One form of diagnostic analysis (see Freeze, 1989) involves the listing of assessment information under five headings: (a) strengths, (b) weaknesses, (c) success patterns, (d) error patterns, and (e) compensatory strategies.

Strengths and weaknesses. Strengths and weaknesses refer to factors which are unrelated to schooling that either facilitate or hinder the teaching learning process. For example, strengths might include: (a) inherent abilities (e.g., physical strength, perfect pitch, a photographic memory, etc.), (b) broad personality characteristics (e.g., friendliness, curiosity, cooperativeness) which largely have developed prior to school or are sustained by social or familial factors outside of school, (c) socio-economic factors (e.g., family wealth which may lead to advantages such as private tutoring or the possession of personal home computer), or (d) advantageous supports outside school (e.g., loving parents willing to work cooperatively with school personnel). Weaknesses might include (a) inherent disabilities (e.g., Down's Syndrome, perceptual impairment, a chronic health impairment, etc.), (b) broad personality characteristics (e.g., physical aggressiveness which may hinder social and academic success at school), (c) socio-economic disadvantages (e.g., poverty or an unstable home life), or (d) a lack of personal supports outside school (e.g., a history of frequent changes of foster home placements).

Success patterns. Success patterns refer to school learning which facilitates achievement.

For individual students or class groups, skills such as fluent reading with comprehension or a clear understanding of place value in mathematics are examples of success patterns. Success patterns may also include pedagogical or environmental factors that facilitate learning. For instance, the use of a well designed text, instructional materials of interest to the students, and continuous evaluation methods that provide frequent corrective feedback are all success patterns. Patterns of behavior, such as following classroom routines, that facilitate learning and social acceptance also are considered to be success patterns.

Error patterns. Error patterns refer to gaps in knowledge and skills, inappropriate, incorrect or incomplete procedures, and misunderstandings that lead to low achievement at school.

For students, they include problems such as an inadequate sight reading vocabulary, difficulties with regrouping in mathematical computations, or inappropriate behaviors that contradict classroom rules or the social norms of their peers.

Inappropriate instructional objectives, uninteresting materials, inconsistent explanations, infrequent and uninformative feedback, and an inhospitable physical environment also are examples of error patterns. Patterns of behavior such as talking out of turn by students or ineffective classroom management by teachers also are considered to be error patterns.

Compensatory strategies. Compensatory strategies primarily refer to the ways students compensate for their weaknesses and error patterns. For instance, a student who uses mnemonics to off-set the affects of a poor memory is using a compensatory strategy. A 'daydreamer' may be compensating for an uninteresting lesson. Widespread off-task behavior in the classroom may mean that the level of instruction is too high or that prior knowledge is lacking. Occassionally, students compensate for strengths or successes. The tall girl who slouches or the 'egghead' who intentionally fails in order to be more like the others are examples.

Case study illustration

To illustrate how the diagnostic analysis is constructed from data-based and curriculum-based information, an assistance request concerning the off-task behavior and poor writing skills of a 9-year-old girl is discussed.

Data-based measurement. Consider, first, an excerpt from a continuous chronologue of the child's in-class behavior (Figure 11.2). This

Figure 11.2   Excerpt from a continuous chronologue

Descriptive Information:	
Student: 'S'	School: 'ABC Elementary'
Teacher: 'T'	School telephone: 123–4567
Observer: Resource Teacher 'O'	Subject Area: Language Arts
Date: Nov. 6 1989	Topic: Personal relationships
Setting: Classroom	Activities: Poems – 'We could be friends'
Level: 4	and 'What Johnny told me'

Time	Antecedent Events	Student Behaviour	Consequences
9:52	T: 'We are going to read two poems about friends. Look at pg. 10. From the picture, what do you think it is about?'	Opens book Looks at wall Looks at friend 'F'	T: ''S'' will you read title for us?
9:53	T: (repeats) ''S'' will you read the title for us?'	S: 'S' 'What?'	Friend 'F' reads the title correctly
9:54	T: ''We could be friends'' – What does this title make you think of?'	'S' Puts up hand then quickly lowers it	Another student is selected and responds
9:56	T: 'Read the poem alone or with a partner'	'S' selects 'F' as her partner, then looks around the room	'F' reads poem alone

excerpt was a part of a series of 30-minute observations during daily language arts instruction. The chronologues pointed to a possible problem with reading that may have contributed to both off-task behavior and writing difficulties. As this excerpt shows, the student (S) relies on a friend (F) to act as a cover for her off-task behavior and to help her out with her academic difficulties.

Consequently, off-task behavior was defined as a target behavior and measured using a behavior sampling measurement strategy (in this case, partial interval time sampling for 15-second intervals over 30-minute observations). The student's off-task behavior is summarized graphically in Figure 11.3.

Curriculum-based measurement. The work sample in Figure 11.4, represents the same student's writing. The work sample was analyzed for success and error patterns at the appropriate curricular level.

Diagnostic analysis. The observational data and work sample information were synthesized in the diagnostic analysis presented in Figure 11.5. The diagnostic analysis was used by the classroom and

120

Figure 11.3   Graph of student's off-task behaviour

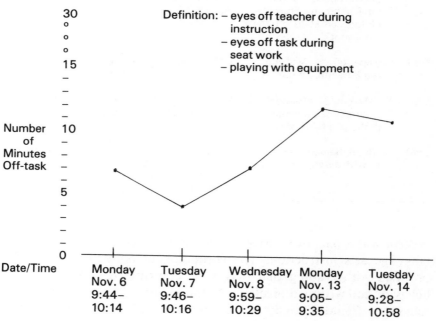

Descriptive Information:

Student: 'S'

Teacher: 'T'

Observer: Resource Teacher 'O'

Date: Nov. 6, 7, 8, 13, 14, 1989

Setting: Classroom

Level: 4

Subject Area: Language Arts

School: 'ABC Elementary'

School telephone: 123–4567

Target: Off-task Behavior

Measurement: Partial interval time
    sampling for 15-second intervals,
    30-minute observations over 5 days

Baseline for off-task behavior

Definition: – eyes off teacher during
                instruction
           – eyes off task during
                seat work
           – playing with equipment

Number of Minutes Off-task

Date/Time

	Monday Nov. 6 9:44– 10:14	Tuesday Nov. 7 9:46– 10:16	Wednesday Nov. 8 9:59– 10:29	Monday Nov. 13 9:05– 9:35	Tuesday Nov. 14 9:28– 10:58

resource teachers to develop a modified programme for the student (illustrated in Figure 11.6).

The data-based and curriculum-based measures developed during the assessment phase of the CC model continued to be used during the implementation of the programme. Typically, modified programs are shared with the student's parents and implemented in the regular classroom with some initial support from the resource teacher until the program is up and running. Other data- and curriculum-based measures such as behavioral recording or curriculum-based testing may be used by the teacher to monitor achievement during the program.

Figure 11.4   Student's writing work sample

Descriptive Information:
Student: 'S'   School: 'ABC Elementary'
Teacher: 'T'   School telephone: 123–4567
Date: Oct. 31 1989   Subject Area: Language Arts
Setting: Classroom   Topic: Descriptive Short story writing
Level: 4   'Hallowe'en'

One day in a grat, grat sematery

in a big, big flower their

lived a little gril. There where lots

of grils in the flowrs. The names of the 7 grils

where Minney, Lowly, Koco, Tufy, Liz, Laty, Paper.

Minney was the first gril too find a grav wish

flowers in frunt of it.

It is important to note that while the original assistance request from the teacher was focused on one child, the modified program developed and implemented by the two teachers involved both child-specific and generic changes. The modified program also involved the classroom teacher in a hands-on professional development activity with respect to writing instruction.

Over the long term, the CC approach is designed to empower teachers with an increasing repertoire of pedagogically sound practices that effectively differentiate instruction in the classroom so that diverse needs can be met.

Third world application

One interesting application of the CC model has been in Trinidad and Tobago where a three-year international development project has been carried out under the auspices of the University of Manitoba, the Canadian International Development Agency, and the Ministry of Education of Trinidad and Tobago (see Rampaul and Freeze, 1990; Rampaul, McCorkell, Freeze and Frith, 1989).

In spite of severe economic constraints, the CC model has been molded to local needs and hundreds of administrators and teachers have been trained in the approach. Many schools now have resource

Figure 11.5   Diagnostic analysis

Descriptive Information:
Student: 'S'   School: 'ABC Elementary'
Teacher: 'T'   School telephone:
Date: Nov 17 1989   123–4567
                                                Subject Area: Language
Level: 4   Arts writing
                                                Target Behaviour: Off-task

Strengths
- eager to please teacher (likes to do chores around classroom)
- has a friend ('F')

Weaknesses
- takes more time than others to get materials, comes in late from recess, etc.
- rarely reads independently
- rarely asks for help when she is having difficulty

Success Patterns
Academic
- indents paragraph
- capitalizes first letter of a sentence
- capitalizes first letter of a proper name
- uses periods at sentence ends
- uses commas between repeated modifiers
- spells single syllable phonically predictable words (e.g., in, a, of, big, lots)
- spells high frequency sight words (e.g., one, day, lived, first, names, find)
- teacher has recently introduced writing conferencing groups
Behavioral
- cooperative
- likes to work in groups
- overall behavior management in classroom is effective

*Error Patterns**
Academic
- no title
- misspells homonyms (e.g., to/too, their/there)
- misspells graphically similar words (e.g. where/were, girl/gril, with/wish)
- misspells words with 'r controlled' vowels (e.g., flowr, sematery, gril)
- unaware 'c' says 's' in front of i, e, and y (e.g., sematery)
- misspells 'final silent e' words (e.g. grav)
- misspells phonically unpredictable words (e.g. grat, frunt)
- story line illogical (e.g. first sentence)
- off-task looking around during instruction and seat work (see graph)
- no procedure in place for correcting spelling
- no modelling of planning/writing/editing process for descriptive short stories
Behavioral
- dependency on 'F' allowed by teacher

Figure 11.5 *continued*

Compensatory Strategies
    Academic
    – repeats modifiers rather than using another one (e.g. big, big)
    – spells by 'sounding-out' unknown words
    Behavioral
    – relies on 'F' to avoid academic work
    – delays tasks by being slow
Comments
    – consider need for reading assessment

---

*These errors were repeated in other work samples.

Figure 11.6 Excerpt (two of four objectives) from a modified program for 'S'

Descriptive Information:
Student: 'S'   School: 'ABC Elementary'
Teacher: 'T'   School telephone: 123–4567
Date: Nov 17 1989   Subject Area: Language Arts writing
Level: 4   Target Behaviour: Staying on-task
Resource Teacher: 'RT'

Objective # 1: Increase on-task behavior.
Content: Eyes on teacher during instruction; eyes on assignment during seat
    work; only authorized talking with peers; no playing with equipment.
Target Date: Dec. 15 1989.
Measurement: Continuation of behavior sampling and graphing (as in
    assessment).
Mastery criteria: 25 out of 30 minutes on-task 5 days in a row.
Methods: (1) Peer ('F') will remind 'S' to 'pay attention' and to 'get back to work'
    when she goes off task.
    (2) Teacher will preview writing lesson with 'S' at 8:55–9:00 am daily.
    Materials and equipment: Behavior sampling form, graph, lesson plans.
    Motivation: (1) On every day that 'S' meets with the criteria for success, she
        will obtain one coupon to cash in when a classroom chore becomes
        available.
    (2) For each 5 minutes 'S' gains on the graph for three days in a row, she and
        'F' will be able to play a spelling game on the computer for 20 minutes.
    Clarification of professional responsibilities: The resource teacher will explain
        the program to 'S' and her peer confederate and attend during the 30
        minutes to monitor behavior during the first week.
        The classroom teacher will conduct the lesson previews, maintain
        measurement and graphing after the first week, and give out the rewards
        when they are earned. The classroom teacher also will initiate and
        maintain contact with the student's parents.
        The resource and classroom teachers will review and adjust the program
        once per week, after the first week, until on-task behavior criteria are
        met.

Figure 11.6 *continued*

Objective # 2: Improve spelling in written work.
Content: (1) proofreading for spelling errors.
    (2) dictionary skills.
    (3) Yes Thomas* visual spelling study program.
Target Dates: (1) Dec. 15 1989, (2) Dec. 15 1989, (3) Mar. 30 1990.
Measurement: (1) proofreading checklist completed for all written assignments,
    (2) dictionary skills checklist completed for all written assignments,
    (3) Yes Thomas* mastery post-test completed.
Mastery criteria: (1) 100% accuracy 10 times in a row,
    (2) 100% accuracy 10 times in a row,
    (3) 90% on Yes Thomas* post-test.
Methods: (1) teach proofreading in resource room to be used in classroom.
    (2) teach dictionary skills in classroom.
    (3) teach Yes Thomas* study method to be monitored by parents at home and by teacher at school.
    (4) complete Yes Thomas* list of most frequently misspelled words up to grade five level in classroom.
Materials and equipment: (1) proofreading skills checklist.
    (2) dictionary skills checklist, dictionary
    (3) Yes Thomas* spelling program.
Motivation: Parents have agreed to buy a bicycle light for 'S' when proofreading and dictionary skills have been mastered to teacher's satisfaction. Teacher has agreed to allow student to use a spelling checker program on the computer after she passes mastery post-test.
Clarification of professional responsibilities: The classroom and resource teachers will team teach in the classroom for 30 minutes per day for three weeks during writing conferencing.
    The resource teacher will demonstrate the teaching of: (1) writing planning, (2) proofreading, (3) editing skills, and (4) dictionary usage in the context of the student writing conferences.
    The classroom teacher will initiate the Yes Thomas* spelling program in classroom for the entire class. The classroom teacher will also coordinate home support for the spelling program with the parents.

---

*Thomas (1979).

programs. One positive effect has been the integration of previously segregated handicapped students into mainstream classrooms in some of those schools. Another has been the introduction of data-based and curriculum-based assessment methods in efforts to improve and guide classroom instruction.

Conclusion

We believe that an in-school special educator working in consultation and collaboration with school staff can help bring about a fundamental reform of teaching practices in the regular classroom in countries with high and moderate living standards.

Data-based and curriculum-based assessment methods can play an important role in making the special educator relevant to the classroom and can provide the glue that holds teachers together in a consultative-collaborative partnership.

References

Ainscow, M. (1990) 'Special Needs in the Classroom: The Development of a Teacher Education Resource Pack', *International Journal of Special Education*, **5**, 1, 13–19.

Bachor, D. and Crealock, C. (1986) *Instructional Strategies for Students with Special Needs*, Scarborough, Ont.: Prentice-Hall Canada.

Bravi, G. (1986) *Support Personnel as Consultants*. Winnipeg, MB: University of Manitoba, Faculty of Education.

Bravi, G. (1988) *The Consultative-collaborative Resource Teacher Program*. Winnipeg, MB: University of Manitoba, Faculty of Education.

Bravi, G. and Freeze, D. R. (1987a) *River East School Division Special Needs Questionnaire: Instructional Aides* (Research Report No. 3). Winnipeg, MB: River East School Division.

Bravi, G. and Freeze, D. R. (1987b) *River East School Division Survey for Teachers of Students in Special Education Programs* (Research Report No. 4). Winnipeg, MB: River East School Division.

Deno, E. N. (1970) 'Special Education as Development Capital', *Exceptional Children*, **37**, 229–37.

Freeze, D. R. (1988) *River East School Division Questionnaire: Parents of Mainstreamed Special Needs Students* (Research Report No. 7). Winnipeg, MB: River East School Division.

Freeze, D. R. (1989) *Achieving*. Winnipeg, MB: Peguis Publishing.

Freeze, D. R. (1990) 'Interviews for Language Arts', *MART Journal*, **9**, 3, 24–9.

Freeze, D. R. and Bravi, G. (1987a) *River East School Division Staff Questionnaire: Low Incidence Mainstreamed Students* (Research Report No. 1). Winnipeg, MB: River East School Division.

Freeze, D. R. and Bravi, G. (1987b) *River East School Division Teacher Questionnaire: Resource Support Services Program* (Research Report No. 2). Winnipeg, MB: River East School Division.

Freeze, D. R. and Bravi, G. (1987c) *River East School Division Child Guidance Clinic Services Questionnaire* (Research Report No. 5). Winnipeg, MB: River East School Divison.

Freeze, D. R. and Bravi, G. (1988) *River East School Division Parent Questionnaire: Resource Program* (Research Report No. 5). Winnipeg, MB: River East School Division.

Freeze, D. R., Bravi, G. and Rampaul, W. (1989) 'Special Education in Manitoba: A Consultative-collaborative Service Delivery Model', in M. Csapo and L. Goguen (Eds), *Special Education Across Canada: Issues and Concerns for the 90s*. Vancouver, B.C.: Center for Human Development and Research.

Gartner, A. and Lipsky, D. K. (1987) 'Beyond Special Education: Toward a Quality System for all Students', *Harvard Educational Review*, **57**, 4, 367–95.

Howell, K. W. and Morehead, M. K. (1987) *Curriculum-based Evaluation for Special and Remedial Education*. Columbus, OH: Charles E. Merrill Publishing.

Kameenui, E. J. and Simmons, D. C. (1990) *Designing Instructional Strategies*. Columbus, OH: Merrill Publishing.

Kerr, M. M. and Nelson, C. M. (1983) *Strategies for Managing Behavior Problems in the Classroom*. Columbus, OH: Charles E. Merrill Publishing.

Langer, J. A. (1981) 'From Theory to Practice: A Pre-reading Plan', *Journal of Reading*, **25**, 2, 152–6.

Mercer, C. D. and Mercer, A. R. (1985) *Teaching Students with Learning Problems*. Columbus, OH: Charles E. Merrill Publishing.

Rampaul, W. and Freeze, D. R. (1990) 'A Consultative-collaborative Resource Teacher Model of Special Education Service Delivery in Trinidad and Tobago'. Paper presented at the International Special Education Congress, Cardiff, Wales, UK.

Rampaul, W., McCorkell, Y., Freeze, D. R. and Frith, E. (1989) 'The Establishment and Operation of Diagnostic Support Resource Centres and the Training of Resource Teachers in Trinidad and Tobago'. Paper presented at International Perspectives: Partnership in Special Education, Vancouver, BC.

Stainback, S. and Stainback, W. (1985) 'The Merger of Special and Regular Education: Can it be Done?', *Exceptional Children*, **51**, 6, 517–21.

Thomas, V. (1979) *Teaching Spelling*, (2nd edn. Toronto, Ont.: Gage Publishing.

Wang, M. C. (1980) 'Adaptive Instruction: Building on Diversity', *Theory into Practice*, **19**, 2, 122–7.

White, O. and Haring, N. (1980) *Exceptional Teaching* (2nd edn.). Columbus, OH: Merrill Publishing.

Wiesinger, R. (1986) 'Disabled Persons in the Third World: Present Situation and Changing Perspectives for the Future', *International Journal of Special Education*, **1**, 1, 21–34.

Zigmond, N., Vallecorsa, A. and Silverman, R. (1983) *Assessment for Instructional Planning in Special Education*. Englewood Cliffs, NJ: Prentice-Hall.

CHAPTER 12

Teacher Appraisal

Ian Petrie and Kath Williams

Introduction

Improving the quality of education and making teachers and schools more accountable are current concerns in many educational systems. For example in France and West Germany teachers are subject to periodic review, and performance evaluation is also widely practised in Australia, Canada and the USA (Pender, 1989). Although Britain lacks a national scheme for evaluating teachers, the 1986 Education Act does include a requirement, not yet implemented, that Local Education Authorities (LEAs) should introduce teacher appraisal. The central purpose of teacher appraisal may be perceived as a managerial move for achieving accountability but there is increasing support for an approach to appraisal which emphasizes professional development and school improvement. Certainly this is a more acceptable emphasis for those professionals who are working in contexts where special educational needs are being addressed.

Teacher appraisal is only one means of fostering development and improvement and should not be considered in isolation. As Bollington, Hopkins and West (1990) point out, its long-term impact on teacher performance will depend upon the extent to which it is integrated with other forms of review and development including headteacher appraisal, whole school review, school development plans, curriculum planning and in-service training (INSET). Nevertheless, there is general acceptance that teacher appraisal must be at the heart of any process of professional development and school improvement. The principle of teacher appraisal is now generally accepted but the prospect of being appraised does cause many teachers

128

anxiety. Certainly the successful implementation of appraisal schemes will depend in large part upon the extent to which teachers' concerns about appraisal are taken into account. This chapter presents some survey findings concerning the views of teachers about appraisal and, using these as a basis, suggests guidelines for the development of an effective and equitable framework acceptable to all teachers.

The background to teacher appraisal in Britain

The demand for the education service to be more open and accountable was increasingly made in the 1960s and early 1970s. By the 1980s the government had come to the firm view that 'regular and formal appraisal of the performance of all teachers is necessary if LEAs are to have the reliable, comprehensive and up-to-date information necessary for the systematic and effective provision of professional support and development and the deployment of staff to best advantage' (DES, 1985, p. 55).

Some pilot studies of teacher appraisal were sponsored by the government in order to provide guidelines for a national scheme, determine what training arrangements were necessary, and assess the financial implications for LEAs and schools. A final report by the National Steering Group (NSG, 1989) was followed by an evaluation of the pilot studies by Bradley *et al.* (1989). Other teacher appraisal schemes initiated by individual LEAs and schools have been discussed by Turner and Clift (1988) and, more recently, a survey of both pilot and non-pilot schemes has been carried out by Her Majesty's Inspectorate (HMI, 1989). The HMI survey emphasizes that the two principal aims of appraisal are to facilitate the professional growth of the individual teacher and to effect institutional improvement.

A framework for appraisal

The National Steering Group has proposed that the appraisal framework should be based on a two-year cycle. This approach (see Figure 12.1) is intended to take into account current pressures on British schools and the need for a continuous process. This proposal, dividing the appraisal process into five stages, has been generally welcomed and can be summarized as follows.

The initial meeting in stage 1 provides the appraiser and appraisee with an opportunity for establishing an agreed understanding of the appraisal framework. For the process of self-appraisal, which follows

Figure 12.1   Components in the appraisal process: a biennial cycle

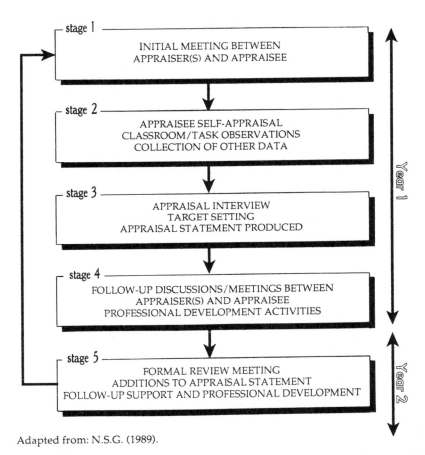

Adapted from: N.S.G. (1989).

in stage 2, ACAS (1986) has recommended that appraisees should examine and reflect upon: the tasks and responsibilities of their current job; those aspects of their job giving most and least satisfaction during the previous year; ways of improving job performance; main aims for the coming year; and career intentions. Another element at this stage, classroom observation, is one which many educationalists believe to be crucial for any scheme. However, there are two major problems. First, agreed criteria as to what constitutes good teaching are lacking, and second, the professional resources required for making observations of real value would be excessive. 'Other data' which might be collected could include the work and progress of pupils and the results of external examinations.

The object of the appraisal interview in stage 3, according to the National Steering Group, is 'to review the appraisee's work, identifying successes and areas which could be developed: to identify any training or development needs; and to agree targets for action' (NSG, 1989, p. 11). For the production of an appraisal statement it is recommended that 'appraisers prepare statements in close consultation with appraisees who should be free to make suggestions as to substance and wording' (p. 12).

The National Steering Group emphasizes the crucial importance of the stage 4 follow-up discussions 'to make sure that action agreed by appraisers and appraisees is pursued' (NSG, 1989, p. 12). The appraisal process in the second year (stage 5) consists entirely of follow-up activities. In fact, as Bollington *et al.* (1990) point out, much of the two-year cycle 'is spent on follow-up work in the form of professional development activities arising from the review process' (p. 11).

The surveys

Our data are derived from two sources. (1) Structured interviews with 32 heads of special schools carried out at the end of the summer term and beginning of the autumn term 1988 (Williams and Petrie, 1989). (2) Questionnaires from 198 respondents (90 secondary, 36 primary, and 72 special school teachers) completed in the spring term of 1989. This sample, largely drawn from teachers attending in-service courses, is clearly not representative. It is also a small sample because teachers at the time, faced with the very heavy demands in the aftermath of the Education Reform Act, clearly felt little enthusiasm for completing questionnaires. However, responding teachers were invited, through open ended questions, to consider a number of issues. These included: the elements of appraisal; the extent of support for appraisal; appraisal and merit awards; appraisal of heads and LEA officers; the consequences of poor appraisal reports; and benefits and disadvantages of appraisal. These questions generated a wide range of responses but, as expected, the views of the special educators and their mainstream colleagues were generally very similar, but where there are differences these are noted.

Elements of appraisal

Teachers were invited to comment about the three major components of teacher appraisal, that is, self-appraisal, classroom observations, and the appraisal interview.

(*a*) *Self-appraisal.* All the respondents regarded self-appraisal as being a valuable part of appraisal and clearly felt that an opportunity to formally reflect upon their own teaching performance was valuable in fostering professional growth. Indeed, some argued that improvement in teaching depends more on self-appraisal than on being appraised by others.

Most respondents felt that the focus of self-appraisal should be preparation and organisation; assessment; record keeping; classroom management and relationships with children and parents.

In this sample the importance of interpersonal relationships was mentioned more often by primary and special school teachers.

(*b*) *Classroom observations.* There was wide agreement that classroom observations should be carried out by heads, deputies or senior teachers. Some teachers wanted external assessors and others wanted appraisees to be given the opportunity to choose their own appraisers, or at least have some say in the choice. Some rejections were very strongly made. For example: 'not the head who has not been in a classroom for five years'; and 'not the head – he's the worst example of a teacher'.

An interesting finding was that a significant minority, and this was particularly true of heads of primary and special schools, argued that formal classroom observations were not necessary and could put a strain on the collaborative, cooperative relationships which are a feature of good schools. A number of respondents suggested that video recordings would provide records of professional activities which could be of value to both appraisers and appraisees and it is surprising that the possibilities of this approach have not been explored more actively.

(*c*) *Appraisal interview.* There was general agreement that the appraisal interview should be conducted by a senior colleague. However, a significant minority wanted appraisal interviews to be conducted by outsiders.

Strong feelings were expressed that it is the appraiser's responsibility to ensure that the interview be conducted in a positive, constructive spirit with emphasis being placed on the appraisee's professional development and that the whole experience should be conducted with sensitivity and tact. One of our respondents, describing an appropriate person to conduct an appraisal interview, wrote 'a trusted, fair-minded colleague'.

Support for appraisal

It seems that the prospect of teacher appraisal is generally accepted but with differing degrees of enthusiasm. However, it was quite striking that those teachers who had experience of appraisal were more positive in their attitude than those who had not. For example one 'experienced' respondent stated: 'Self-assessment linked to a third party's observations and constructive criticism are to be welcomed'. Most respondents felt that teacher appraisal would improve the quality of teaching as long as it was positive and backed by adequate resources. However, a minority were not at all convinced. One respondent, for example, wrote: 'Very, very minimally – the answer is to improve salaries'. Furthermore, the acceptance of appraisal by many teachers depended upon a number of conditions being met. For example, one teacher replied: 'Yes but only if the appraiser is perceived by the appraisee as a competent and effective teacher and it is conducted on a friendly basis'.

Some of the replies, again particularly from heads, pointed out that teacher appraisal was only one element among a number which could improve the quality of teaching. Others included the provision of adequate resources, teacher support and training, and staff commitment and loyalty.

Appraisal and merit awards

Almost all respondents rejected, many vehemently, the idea that merit awards might be made on the basis of appraisals. 'No – how can there be trust, integrity and genuine personal development if this is implemented', is a typical response. However, a few respondents found some virtue in the suggestion. For example: 'They could be part of the basis'. 'Within limits, yes. Why pay passengers for doing as little as possible?'. However, very few respondents supported in full the notion of salaries being linked to appraisal.

Consequences of poor appraisal reports

There was unanimous agreement that teachers should be able to appeal/complain against poor appraisal reports. One respondent wrote: 'Personal differences and professional disagreements may be operating and this can be particularly prevalent in the small school'. If this view is correct then special schools will be more at risk in this respect.

A number of respondents argued that if the appraisal is a positive experience, and if the final 'report' is a negotiated, agreed statement, then this problem should not arise. However, although the National Steering Group proposes that a formal complaints procedure relating to appraisal should be established, it does not go so far as to advocate that the content of the appraisal statement should be subject to the agreement of the appraisee. The insistence of our respondents that teacher appraisal should be positive and supportive is most apparent when they consider the consequences of unsatisfactory appraisal reports. There is widespread recognition that there may be a point in time when redeployment for an individual teacher may be necessary but before that stage is reached help should be readily available. This help was described by respondents in terms of advice, counselling, guidance, support, training and analyses of teaching problems.

Bottom-up appraisal procedures

Some heads, deputies and senior teachers doubted whether junior staff members had the necessary background knowledge to appraise their seniors. However, most of our sample, and this included the majority of senior management, thought junior staff should appraise their seniors. As one head of a special school said: 'This would be equitable and could be very useful'.

Appraisal of heads and LEA officers

A number of respondents thought that heads should set the pace in implementing appraisal. For example, one special school head said: 'As a head I feel I would lack credibility if I were not first in the hot seat'.

The question of who should appraise heads produced conflicting answers. Some respondents thought LEA advisers or officers would be most appropriate. However, an equal number suggested fellow heads should be given the task. It is hardly surprising that many heads should want their prospective appraisers to have had headship experience and this is recommended by the National Steering Group. Nor is it surprising that some assistant teachers would welcome the opportunity of making a contribution towards the appraisal of heads.

Many respondents felt that the appraisal process of LEA officers and advisory staff should include some input from schools.

Confidentiality of appraisal records

Most of our respondents anticipated the recommendation of the National Steering Group that the availability of appraisal reports 'should be restricted to the appraisee, the appraiser(s), the headteacher of the school, the CEO of the LEA and any LEA officer or adviser specifically designated by him or her' (NSG, 1989, p. 17).

Advantages of appraisal

The expectation was that all respondents would be able to specify some advantages of appraisal. However, a significant minority, about 11 per cent of our questionnaire sample, saw no benefits at all in teacher appraisal.

Negative responses, some of which were quite tart, included: 'None', and 'I am waiting for someone to stand up and be counted in defence of your grassroots, hardworking, chalkface teacher who shares little of the monetary and educational rewards other than the responses they get from the children they teach'.

The majority of respondents (nearly 90 per cent) did recognise that there were advantages to teacher appraisal. Those listed included: identifying the needs of individual teachers; identifying in-service training (INSET) needs; building confidence in teachers; encouragement to improve performance; and indicating to teachers that they are noticed, are important and it matters what they do.

Disadvantages of appraisal

As expected, all respondents could identify possible disadvantages/dangers in teacher appraisal. In general the disadvantages revolved around: personality clashes; biased judgements; the generation of ill-feeling among colleagues; and appraisees feeling threatened. The following are examples of individual responses.

  (i) 'The terminology is threatening – it is coming at a time of low morale, high stress, financial cuts, governor power, etc.'.
  (ii) 'If it is not well resourced and sensitively handled a lot of damage could result'.
  (iii) 'It could be interpreted as punitive, it could be abused to victimize

individuals, it could become divisive, it could intimidate'.
(iv) 'As it is unlikely that adequate funding and time will go into any appraisal procedure adopted it is likely to have major faults'.
(v) 'Teachers feeling and *being* threatened; teachers feeling and *being* compared; teachers teaching to suit the head – who may be *wrong*; teachers being judged *unfairly* and condemned *wrongly*'.

It should be noted that these five respondents, in spite of their anxieties and reservations, all saw overall value in the process of teacher appraisal and were in favour of it being implemented.

Conclusions from the survey

A majority of respondents, both special needs teachers and their mainstream colleagues, clearly accept that the formal and systematic appraisal of teachers would improve the quality of teaching. Nevertheless, it is significant that all our respondents identified possible problems and disadvantages with appraisal and it is essential, therefore, that these anxieties and concerns should be addressed.

Guidelines for appraisal

The appraisal literature and data from these surveys suggest that the following guidelines are crucial for the development of professionally acceptable appraisal schemes.

(i) The introduction of formal teacher appraisal should be carefully planned, be preceded by staff consultations and negotiation, with the aim of producing an agreed scheme. Teacher appraisal is more likely to be accepted if it develops from a process of decision-making in which all teachers have been included.
(ii) The focus of appraisal in education should be formative, emphasizing professional development, support and in-service training needs. Any managerial requirements for dealing with irremedial incompetence should be dealt with quite separately.
(iii) Appraisers and appraisees require training and appraisers need to be sensitive and empathic and held in high regard and professional respect by the appraisee. An agreed outcome to the appraisal process should be sought but can only be achieved if the appraiser-appraisee relationship is a positive one.
(iv) Both 'top-down' and 'bottom-up' procedures should be employed in professional appraisals. This is not merely a matter of equity but also of efficiency.
(v) Cooperative and collaborative teaching are highly regarded in many

educational programmes, particularly when special needs are being met, and schemes of teacher appraisal should be designed to foster these approaches rather than threaten them.

(vi) The current emphasis being given to teacher appraisal should not obscure the necessity for all professionals in the educational services to be appraised. Furthermore, the appraisal of individuals should be supplemented by the evaluation of institutions and services.

Nisbet (1986, p. 15) has succinctly pointed the way forward for teacher appraisal:

> It should be linked to a developmental programme which will provide support to improve staff performance. It must not damage or distort the processes of learning and teaching. It must not damage morale, destroy relationships and trust, discourage initiative or diminish the whole-hearted spontaneous and unforced commitment which many teachers give to their work far beyond the call of duty.

References

ACAS (1986) *Report of the Appraisal/Training Group*. London: ACAS.

Bollington, R., Hopkins, D. and West, M. (1990) *An Introduction to Teacher Appraisal*. London: Cassell.

Bradley, H. W., *et al.* (1989) *Report on the Evaluation of the School Teacher Appraisal Pilot Study*. Cambridge: CIE.

DES (1985) *Better Schools*. London: HMSO.

HMI (1989) *Development in the Appraisal of Teachers*. London: DES.

NSG (National Steering Group for Teacher Appraisal) (1989) *School Teacher Appraisal – A National Framework*. London: HMSO.

Nisbet, J. (1986) 'Appraisal for Improvement', in Stones, E. and Wilcox, B. (Eds) *Appraising Appraisal*. Birmingham: BERA.

Pender, K. (1989) *Staff Development. The Issues Involved and a Suggested Model*. Occasional Paper No. 17. Liverpool: University of Liverpool, Department of Education.

Turner, G. and Clift, P. (1988) *Studies in Teacher Appraisal*. London: Falmer Press.

Williams, K. and Petrie, I. (1989) 'Teacher Appraisal in Special Schools', *British Journal of Special Education*, **16**, 2, 53–6.

CHAPTER 13

Classroom Assistants: Staff Development Issues

Maggie Balshaw

This chapter addresses the issue of the provision of in-service training for assistants working with children with special educational needs in mainstream schools in one English local authority. It does this through briefly looking at background issues, and through an examination of the training provided by the authority. It evaluates this training, identifies the positive aspects and pinpoints the weaknesses. Through some aspects found whilst examining the wider contexts in which assistants work, it offers some wider comments for consideration. It is based on ongoing research that began over two years ago and involves a variety of methods of investigation.

Background

I first became interested in this subject as long ago as 1986 when first appointed into my role with Cambridgeshire Local Education Authority (LEA) as coordinator for special needs. My accountabilities included the in-service training programmes for special educational needs staff. This included the assistants the authority was employing to work in mainstream schools, for the specific support of children with special educational needs. There had been a number of responses in Britain to the 1981 Education Act in terms of provision of services and the appointment of assistants was an aspect of this changed focus. These responses represented a move away from an emphasis on categories, care and segregation towards a concern with needs, curriculum and integration, in the ethos of the post-Warnock era (Ainscow and Muncey, 1989).

A search of the literature into the subject of the training and deployment of non-qualified assistants working in mainstream classrooms reveals that little is written of it except in the positivist stance. Published studies tend to deal with pre-test and post-test scores of assistant 'performance' before and after experiencing in-service training (INSET) (e.g. Farrell and Sugden, 1984, Gillis-Olion and Olion, 1985). In the USA, Pickett (1986) and Orford (1989) detailed some issues about the need for certification and a career structure, and clear job descriptions for assistants (or paraprofessionals as they are known in the USA). Frith and Lindsey (1982) echoed some of these findings. In the UK, Woolf and Bassett (1988) had made similar recommendations for assistants in special schools. A study carried out by Mortimer (1989) bore this out. Amongst her recommendations were that accountabilities should be clear, permanent contracts should be issued, and that basic in-service training should be available to all assistants.

In Britain there have been varying responses by LEAs to the issues of training assistants. The two most widely documented are OPTIS 'Working Together' (Oxfordshire) and SAINTS (Wiltshire) (Burnham et al., 1988, and Clayton, 1989, detail their aims and contents). These are differing approaches and each differs considerably from those made by Cambridgeshire.

The training courses offered in Cambridgeshire to date have trained at least 400 assistants working in mainstream schools and these courses are structured in such a way as to offer two levels of experience.

The Level 1 introductory course aims to provide, over ten weekly sessions of two and a half hours, an overview of areas which assistants will find useful when taking up post or when having minimum experience. The 'menu' includes responses to the 1981 Education Act – policy and provision, the assistant's role in that context and in school, and 'skills' aspects such as speech and language development, physiotherapy, music therapy, behaviour management, microcomputer programs, occupational therapy and art and craft. A school visit is also included.

The Level 2 courses offer specific areas of interest which in the evaluation of the first Level 1 courses assistants picked out as priorities for further training. These are supporting the secondary curriculum; behaviour management; team development; speech and language development; motor skills; micro-computer applications and programs; and observation and assessment in the classroom. This Level 2 system is modular. In order to achieve a full Level 2 certificate, assistants have to attend four modules of their choice (60 hours attendance).

The courses have been offered county-wide in various Educational Development Centres by teams of people coordinated by a small steering group. Evaluation of these courses by the assistants themselves has been part of the data used to tease out what are the important issues for LEAs and schools to address. In addition to this information, working sessions with assistants on INSET courses have made it possible to gather a great deal of further information about their perceptions of both the INSET and other forms of support they receive. It also gave a wealth of very useful information about their working conditions in school and how they feel about them. The insights provided by these have made it possible to build up a picture for further investigation which has been carried out through in-depth interviews with a small number of assistants, working in nursery, primary and secondary mainstream schools.

What was found out

The information gathered and the analysis of it has led to conclusions about the following issues:

(a) the benefits gained from the INSET experiences
(b) the limitations of the INSET support as provided
(c) the experiences assistants described in terms of their working contexts and how there are potential areas for training which so far have not been explored in any formal or extensive way.

Findings with respect to these three areas are as follows.

(a) *The benefits*

Increased confidence. There is no doubt that participating in INSET had increased the assistants' confidence in a number of ways. A particular aspect of this was increased confidence in asserting what they felt was reasonable in terms of their working conditions.

Increased skills. There was evidence of assistants feeling prepared to deal with certain skill areas, such as supporting teachers in secondary curriculum areas or working with children with language difficulties.

Meeting other assistants. Although it was not *the* major perceived target at the outset, this seemed to be equally if not more important than acquiring confidence and skills for many people. However much time was apportioned to discussion and shared experiences, this seemed not to be enough! Comparisons, favourable and unfavourable, were offered about 'delivery' modes and interactive modes employed by course leaders/tutors.

Identifying further needs. In all the evaluation of courses (verbal feedback or written forms) there were comments about certain aspects which could well be taken up as either training or management issues.

(b) *The limitations*

'Relevance'. The difficulty of 'pleasing all of the people all of the time' was evident throughout the analysis of the assistants' comments. Although assistants were grateful for the opportunity to attend the courses, particularly with the introductory course, they felt that large proportions of it were 'not for me' – not while 'I'm working in the way that I am at the moment with this child or particular group of children'. This of course applied to different sessions of the course for different people!

'Relationships'. Not enough emphasis was placed on how to work with other adults (with the exception of the team development module). This seemed to be a very real need as expressed by the assistants. 'Ground rules' in adult relationships and related roles and how to establish them was an expressed need.

'Resentment'. Although this was much played down it cannot be ignored. Many of the assistants, being part-time, were doing INSET in their own time, and it was not giving them any extra pay to be so qualified. Furthermore because they are mostly on temporary contracts there was no perceived career structure for doing it. It was acknowledged that most people were doing INSET to make them feel better and more confident at their jobs, but there was a continuing and relentless 'niggle' about where it was getting them.

(c) *The experiences in context*

There was extensive evidence that teachers were neither prepared nor trained to manage assistants in their classrooms, and that the management of schools in many cases had not addressed this issue.

The assistants described numerous instances of feeling 'left out' of the communication system at various levels. The most serious aspect was that of being sent to somebody's classroom and the teacher being unaware that they were to arrive, much less aware of what to do about it when they did.

Confusion reigned and there was great ambiguity over the aims, ethos and provision for special educational needs in schools. The assistants were experiencing and learning one thing in one situation and sometimes very different things in other contexts within their own school, whilst often having heard the LEA stance in INSET contexts.

Many assistants expressed the feeling that they needed more support. At a pastoral level this was particularly lacking where there was only one assistant working in the school. Lack of support in talking over difficulties they were experiencing was quite widespread, this often being expressed in terms of lack of time during their working hours. Some instances of their being put in difficult positions (e.g., with parents) without clear guidance and nobody with whom to discuss it, were noted.

These then seem to be the major issues which need addressing. They are summed up by the comments of two assistants. One said, 'I feel like piggy in the middle', whilst another, in contrast, noted, 'We work as a team very much'. Clearly great differences in practice do exist. It *is*, however, possible to achieve the positive end of the spectrum. By careful preparation, management and support it *should* be possible to move from the first statement to the second.

The implications and recommendations

The areas of concern described led to the conclusion that the effective-ness of training and support for assistants need to be examined very critically and that the LEA and schools have two major issues to address. These are to do with LEA INSET and 'in-house' staff development.

(i) *LEA INSET*

The first issue is concerned with what may be done to improve the present structure of INSET courses, particularly whilst the assistants continue to be centrally funded under Local Management of Schools. I would offer the following advice to my own LEA and tentatively to other LEAs where it is perceived to be relevant, as a result of what I have learnt. There is a need for:

- a more accurate match in terms of content and the needs of the perceived target groups, perhaps through more optional sessions within the framework of a course
- an increase in the time assistants spend discussing their working lives in order to derive mutual support and guidance. This should involve a specific focus such as the review of their own working practice; the school's philosophy and provision for special educational needs; how assistants deal with parental contact
- an increase in the training which can be offered to teachers and assistants to work together
- a changed emphasis from skills needed for working with children to those needed for working with other adults
- a method of capitalising on the in-service training received which eliminates temporary contracts and 'losing' a trained assistant from the system.

(ii) 'In-house' staff development

Secondly, there is a need for 'in-house' staff training involving not only assistants but all the staff in the school. An 'outside' system of training cannot begin to address the issues which are influenced by the specific ethos, organisation and practice of each school. Therefore the *only* effective way to address them is 'in-house' staff development.

I wish to propose six principles derived from the analysis of the differing contexts in which assistants work. In presenting them I will include some examples of the evidence which has convinced me that these principles are so important. The six principles are:

Classroom assistants should:

(i) know exactly what their role and responsibilities are and be involved in regularly reviewing and monitoring them;
(ii) understand and be part of the communication system in the school;
(iii) be seen positively as part of a range of provision for meeting special needs by all members of school staff;
(iv) be part of the school team and regarded as partners in team development;
(v) be encouraged to examine their personal skills, and do this in collaboration with the team, in order to capitalise on these;
(vi) examine, with colleagues, their needs for development and training, and receive support in the school for meeting these needs.

I will consider each of these principles in more detail.

(i) *Classroom assistants should know exactly what their role and responsibilities are, and be involved in regularly reviewing and monitoring them.*

I found that assistants who worked within a clearly defined structure, knowing what their responsibilities were, and that they were playing an active part in reviewing how their job was going, had a greater sense of satisfaction and productivity. The difference this can make was described by an assistant in this way:

> What we do, we discuss at the end of term and at the beginning of the year and get our rota of how we're going to work, and then discuss it with the class teachers – we have meetings every day. I was absolutely amazed last week on the course when the other people didn't know, really didn't know, what was expected of them and thought that must be very difficult.

(ii) *Classroom assistants should understand and be part of the communication system in the school.*

The fact that assistants often work part-time means special care should be taken to make sure they are in touch with what is going on in the school. Even if they work full-time steps should be taken in order that they feel part of the overall plan. It is unreasonable to expect assistants to give of their best in the following situations:

> Even now I go into a classroom and I have no idea what that lesson is going to be about. How can I get anything ready if I've had no response from the teacher?

If people coming into the school, for example parents, are not included in the communication system about the assistants, then the following can happen: 'Oh, so you're the general dogsbody!'. This was said by a parent after inquiring why an assistant was in the classroom. As the assistant said afterwards, 'I was very upset about that!'.

(iii) *Classroom assistants should be seen positively as part of a range of provision for meeting special needs by all members of school staff.*

The school needs to be clear about its vision and purpose with regard to special needs. Furthermore this should translate itself into clarity and consistency of practice. The kinds of attitude adopted by staff to forms of provision, including assistants, need to be examined and the aims for the work done together agreed as a common purpose. If this is achieved then the whole of the type of experience outlined in the following statement is unlikely:

> The English teacher I've worked with has been very helpful, she has been very nice as a person, because some of the staff won't accept us for what we are (assistants), if they could be 100% honest, don't want us in the classroom!

(iv) *Classroom assistants should be part of the school team and regarded as partners in team development.*

Developing an agreed set of purposes within the ethos of a set of common aims which have been clarified and devised by the team is a way of encouraging more involvement, commitment and understanding. The assistant(s) should be seen as part of this developing team, involved in the decision-making process at the appropriate level about what they are going to do. This assistant expressed the value she had found in this experience in the following way:

> We work as a team very much, and I am allowed a lot of freedom which I must say I do like. I like to be able to feel I'm actually thinking for myself, albeit I can always talk it over with the teacher.

(v) *Classroom assistants should be encouraged to examine their personal skills, and do this in collaboration with the team, in order to capitalise on these.*

Capitalising on the skills and talents assistants have is an area which schools should address. There was considerable evidence of wasted talents and time in the assistants' analyses of their deployment. As one assistant said:

> I feel that because I've got children of their age I understand them. I see a lot more than the staff do, of what goes on in the classroom and how they react.

She went on to say that all this knowledge could be used more positively, given the opportunity. The school should provide a sure and safe environment to examine both strengths and weaknesses, which can be openly acknowledged and discussed and accounted for.

Support for assistants who have difficulties in some areas should be provided at pastoral level.

(vi) *Classroom assistants should examine, with colleagues, their needs for development and training, and receive support in the school for meeting these needs.*

Schools should encourage assistants to examine their INSET needs. These needs and the school's needs for their work should be incorporated into the staff development programme. Many of these issues can and should be addressed in school, otherwise support for them to attend externally provided training should be given, and this *within* their working hours. The sort of situation described here would then be avoided:

> I went on a Wednesday afternoon, and I don't normally work on Wednesday afternoons! I gave that up out of my own time to go on the course, and I think that in a way if you've taken time to do this it might be recognised somewhere along the line . . .

In conclusion

It seems then, that the three major issues which have been identified as a result of the research reported in this chapter are that

(1) there are benefits and limitations to LEA-organised in-service courses, and LEAs could well take note of these;
(2) there are a large number of contextual 'in-house' issues about the management of assistants which should be addressed;
(3) there are six statements of principle which I have identified that might help schools to address these in-house issues.

It is clear that issues 2 and 3 should be addressed for the reasons I have outlined. Furthermore, the six statements of principle should be seen as part of an overall policy for staff development. This should involve staff in developing personally and professionally as part of a team which reviews its practice in a collaborative way.

With this argument in mind, I would recommend a form of 'collaborative enquiry' into the practices of a school, using the outcomes constructively to plan improvements in this practice. In *Help in the Classroom* (Balshaw, 1991) the practical frameworks necessary for carrying out a collaborative inquiry of this nature are outlined.

Collaborative inquiry requires all those involved to be learners together about their work. This means starting with perceptions, attitudes and philosophy, going on to address planning, strategies and action, and using in-built procedures for monitoring and evaluating what they are doing together. In this way the individual needs of their children, no matter how diverse, have a much better chance of being met.

References

Ainscow, M. and Muncey, J. (1989) *Meeting Individual Needs*. London: David Fulton Publishers.

Balshaw, M.H. (1991) *Help in the Classroom*. London: David Fulton Publishers.

Burnham, M., Brayton, H. and Deans, M. (1988) *Working Together*. Oxford: OPTIS, Oxford Polytechnic.

Clayton, W.T. (1989) 'Induction Courses for Special Welfare Assistants', *Special Children*, **30**, May.

Farrell, P. and Sugden, M. (1984) 'An Evaluation of an EDY Course in Behavioural Techniques for Classroom Assistants in a School for Severe Learning Difficulties', *Educational Psychology*, **4**, 3, 185–98.

Frith, G.H. and Lindsey, J. (1982) 'Certification, Training and other Programming Variables Affecting Special Education and the Paraprofessional Concept', *The Journal of Special Education*, **16**, 229–36.

Gillis-Olion, M. and Olion, L. (1985) 'Preparing Early Childhood Educators and Paraprofessionals to Work with Mainstreamed Handicapped Children', *Early Childhood Development and Care*, **21**, Part 4, 291–304.

Mortimer, B. (1989) 'Life with the Paraprofessionals', *Times Educational Supplement*, 13 Oct.

Orford, S. (1989) 'Special Needs in Los Angeles', *Support for Learning*, **4**, 1, 36–45.

Pickett, A.L. (1986) 'Certified Partners: Four Good Reasons for the Certification of Paraprofessionals', *American Educator*, **10**, Part 3, 31–47.

Woolf, M. and Bassett, S. (1988) 'How Classroom Assistants Respond', *British Journal of Special Education*, **15**, 2, 62–4.

CHAPTER 14

Videocourses: A Modern Solution to an Age-old Problem

Roy McConkey and Alice Bradley

Overview

In developing countries, the dearth of trainers could be overcome through the use of ready-made training packages. This chapter describes the development and evaluation of packages based around video programmes made in Zimbabwe and Malaysia. These video-courses are aimed primarily at untrained staff in education, health and social welfare services but they are also suited for use with family members and community helpers. The viability of the approach has been tested in a range of settings and with three different styles of training packages – one which examines the lifestyle of the person with a mental handicap, a second on nurturing the development of pre-school children, and the third on teaching techniques. This approach is also well suited to meeting the training demands arising in the developed world from dispersed community-based services for people with severe learning difficulties.

The task

Throughout the world, an estimated 50 million people are thought to have severe learning difficulties (mental handicap). During the past 20 years there have been striking advances in our ability to prevent their disabilities becoming too much of a handicap. As a World Health Organization report (1985) noted, 'most of the recent advances in education and training, and in helping mentally retarded persons to develop their skills, are comparatively simple and these techniques can be acquired after only a short period of training by most people irrespective of their previous experience'. The challenge, the report states, is 'to devise a strategy for disseminating existing knowledge and skills to the hundreds of thousands of people who come into daily contact with mentally retarded people' (p.7).

This task is no less urgent in industrialised countries where there is increasing emphasis placed on integrating pre-schoolers, children, teenagers and adults into mainstream education, employment, leisure and housing. The goal of providing individually tailored services in community settings cannot be achieved if there is a continued reliance on existing 'specialist' models of training. A comparison between these specialist models and those required by community services shows marked contrasts:

Contrasts between 'Community' and 'Specialist' Training Models

Community training	Specialist training
● Open to all	● Selective
● Client-centred	● Professional qualifications
● Dispersed services	● Congregated services
● Available locally	● Available centrally

Traditional training models are geared towards segregated, specialist services in which professionals are expected to cope with a diversity of clients with multi-various needs. Adaptations of the specialist model, such as modularisation and reformulation of courses as distance-learning packages is *not* the solution; rather, a radically different approach is required.

A new approach

The characteristics of a new training approach can be summarised as follows:

● *Front-line helpers* are the main consumers – i.e., 'untrained' service staff, families and community workers. Their levels of literacy are likely to be poor, hence the emphasis needs to be on learning by seeing and doing rather than from talks and books (Werner and Bower, 1982).

- They need to be given information that is *practical and relevant* to their needs. Examples of good practice occurring in their culture and under similar conditions to those they experience are likely to be the most useful. Hence indigenously produced materials are necessary (Thornburn and Roeher, 1986).

- The training must take place *locally* and it should be *easily repeated* for differing groups within the community and over time as new people come along. Trainees have many other commitments in their homes and community which make it impossible for them to travel even if they could afford it. Given the dearth of experienced trainers in most countries, some form of distance-learning programme will be required (Thornburn, 1990).

- The training must help to *develop better services*. Too often training is divorced from service goals by focusing on acquiring knowledge and developing skills. Models of training also need to embrace methods for changing attitudes, planning service goals and nurturing partnerships among the stake-holders (Cullen, 1988).

Videocourses

The concept of a videocourse attempts to embrace all these aspirations. It consists of a series of specially-made video programmes based around a particular theme, for example play activities for the pre-school years. The programmes are recorded in local settings – homes, day centres, residences and neighbourhoods, and feature staff, parents and siblings engaged with children or adults with special needs. The advent of battery-operated video equipment (camcorders) enables filming to be done in the remotest of areas (McConkey, 1990).

Advantages

The advantages of video as a learning medium can be summarised as follows:

- portrays the viewer's world
- overcomes literacy problems
- commentaries in local languages can be added
- information is packaged
- programmes are transportable and repeated
- enhances status of people with disabilities.

The last point is especially significant in the developing world. Featuring devalued people on video and showing them succeeding at tasks has been shown to induce more positive attitudes in viewers (Donaldson and Martinson, 1977).

Possible disadvantages of video – equipment breakdowns and unavailability of parts – have not proved to be a problem. Prices have dropped considerably in recent years and service engineers can now be found in nearly all countries. Super VHS has been our choice of video format as this gives superior picture quality with portability.

A videocourse usually has about five programmes, each around 20 minutes long. Course participants will view one programme per session, with time between sessions to try out the ideas shown.

Video used alone has three disadvantages as shown below but can be supplemented by other means to help overcome these:

Video cannot provide	Supplements
● Knowledge into practice	● Activities
● Reference	● Handbooks
● Individual Help	● Tutors

Course handbook

A videocourse package also includes a handbook which summarises the main points made in the course, provides suggestions for further learning activities, and gives guidance on the practical exercises which participants undertake. These handbooks are illustrated with black and white photographs and/or cartoons and although written first in English, the handbooks should be translated to local languages.

Tutor groups

Videocourses are designed to be taken by a group of people under the guidance of a local tutor. The advantages of groups, and the role of tutor can be summarised thus:

Advantages of groups	Role of tutor
● Time effective	● Issue invitations
● People share their experiences	● Organise equipment
● Enables partnerships to develop	● Introduce topic and key learning points

● Encourages
completion of
activities   ● Facilitate discussion

Tutors are drawn from available service personnel. No prior training
or experience in leading groups has been necessary but two-day
training workshops are held for potential course tutors to introduce
them to the package and to train them for their role. Fundamental to
the approach is the interactive and experiential elements of the training
process.

Evaluation

Various videocourses were developed and evaluated in Ireland,
including 'Putting Two Words Together', 'Let's Play', 'Let's Talk'
and 'Count Me In'. Significant improvements were found in course
participants' styles of interactions with children who also showed
increased competence (McConkey, 1988).

In 1985, two videocourses were produced in Zimbabwe in association with Zimcare Trust. 'More Than Care' focused on children and
young adults with severe and multiple handicaps, showing how their
physical, social and cognitive development could be nurtured and their
competencies in self-care increased (McConkey and Templer, 1987).
The course consisted of six 20-minute programmes, filmed in a
hospital residence and a 56-page illustrated course handbook. The
table below shows the reactions of over 100 course participants. Each
component was rated on a three point scale – not useful, useful, very
useful. One of the components was selected as the most useful.

Reactions to the 'More Than Care' Videocourse

Course components	% Rating VERY Useful	% Rating MOST Useful
Video	88	48
Talks	67	13
Activities	63	24
Making equipment	63	7
Group discussions	61	4
Handbooks	55	3
Checklists/Forms	49	2

Developing videocourses

The feasibility and efficacy of this training model are now well-established. The task is primarily one of producing further courses. The steps involved can be summarised as follows:

1. Identification of needs. For developing countries this stage must be done in association with local personnel who are actively engaged in service delivery. This is essential for the sustainability of the endeavour (Ager, 1990). The aims of the videocourse will begin to emerge at this point.

2. Identification of content. The 'teaching' messages to be conveyed by the course are listed. Settings for video-recordings are researched, usually places where examples of good practice are to be found.

3. Initial recordings. As recordings are undertaken in centres and homes, further examples of good practice are invariably encountered. The content and aims of the videocourse become further refined in discussions with service personnel.

4. Production of 'pilot' version. The scripting and editing of the video programmes requires quite an investment of time; roughly one hour per minute of finished programme. With modern Super VHS equipment, however, passable programmes can be made using home recorders. A draft of the course handbook is also prepared at this stage.

5. Training workshops for tutors. A two-day training workshop is held for people who might tutor the course, usually personnel working in services as managers, specialists, trainers, etc. The workshop not only introduces them to the aims and content of the course but enables them to experience and practise important group leader skills. Afterwards the tutors are expected to organise at least one course in their local area. The pilot materials are made available to the tutors at little or no cost.

6. Evaluation of course. Tutors are encouraged to try the course with the different participants – staff, parents, community helpers – and feedback about the course is obtained from tutors and participants. This is mainly through opinion questionnaires.

7. Revisions and translations. The course is revised in light of feedback and the final version made available for sale to a wider audience. In order to keep costs to a minimum, an English version of the package is sold with free translation rights in any other language. Instructions are provided as to how a translated commentary can be dubbed on to the tapes.

We hasten to add though, that this seven-stage schema is an idealised version of how videocourses are produced. Our reality is that we move up and down among the stages as the process unfolds. For example, the aims might be revised in the light of the try-outs. Indeed such flexibility is necessary if the course is to address the needs of the consumers.

Examples of videocourses

Initially our videocourses focused mainly on 'teaching' techniques for use with children who had mental handicaps, for instance play activities and games to encourage manual dexterity, socialisation and use of language. 'Let's Talk' (McConkey and Price, 1986) and 'Living and Learning' (see Table 14.1) are two examples. In each instance, the videocourse provides a 'developmental curriculum' of possible learning experiences.

There is undoubtedly a great need for further programmes of this sort, especially if we are to comprehensively cover all the competencies which children and young adults need to acquire. However, these might be conceived as 'second-level' courses in that they presuppose participants have clarified what they are aiming to achieve. Latterly we have experimented with other styles of videocourse.

'A Better Life' (see Table 14.1) might be considered a 'first-level' course as it encourages participants to explore the lifestyle of persons with a mental handicap. This course was inspired by the Open University Package, 'Mental Handicap: Patterns for Living'. Other first-level courses might focus on integrated education, employment training and so forth.

A 'third level' course, 'Teaching Skills', modelled on the EDY programmes (McBrien and Foxen, 1987) has recently been evaluated in Malaysia. A feature of such courses is that they provide participants with generic training skills which can be applied across various curricula. Other courses at this level could cover counselling skills and conversational skills.

The distinction into first, second and third level courses is a further test of the versatility of the video-based training model but also clarifies the training curriculum offered to participants when a range of courses are available, although admittedly such days are still far off.

154

Table 14.1   Examples of videocourses developed in Malaysia

'A BETTER LIFE' *for people with a mental handicap*	'LIVING AND LEARNING' *for pre-schoolers and children with multiple handicaps*	'TEACHING SKILLS VIDEOCOURSE'
AIMS	AIMS	AIMS
• to change people's expectations • to illustrate good practice • to evaluate present services • to identify new opportunities • to build networks of helpers	• to give an understanding of early development • to observe children's abilities • to learn new ideas • to work together with other people	• the need for appropriate and relevant goals • to illustrate five basic teaching techniques • peer review of teaching practices
CONTENTS	CONTENTS	CONTENTS
1. Introduction to the Course 2. A Family Life 3. A Homely Life 4. A Meaningful Life 5. A Community Life 6. A Working Life 7. An Enjoyable Life 8. A Shared Life	1. Introducing the Series 2. Learning to Move 3. Learning about People 4. Learning to Think 5. Learning to be Independent	1. An Introduction to Teaching Skills 2. Modelling 3. Prompting 4. Feedback 5. Chaining 6. Favourable Learning Conditions
TARGET AUDIENCES	TARGET AUDIENCES	TARGET AUDIENCES
• Staff joining services/staff in service • Community – Volunteers • Families	• Families • Staff in services • Volunteer helpers	• Staff in services • Volunteer helpers • Families

Conclusions

The needs of services in the developing world for new models of training have stimulated the development of new approaches. Ironically the need can be just as great in the developed world as we begin to address the issues raised by the expansion of community-based services, in particular the training opportunities made available to parents, community helpers and staff newly recruited to services with no previous experience. From our experiences as trainers in Britain we are confident that the videocourse model has much to offer services in industrialised countries as well as the developing world.

Acknowledgements

The work reported in this chapter has been suported by grants from Irish Foreign Aid, Cheshire Homes International and the British Overseas Development Administration. We gratefully acknowledge the contribution of our colleagues in Malaysia – Sarah Holloway and Diana Khoo, and in Zimbabwe of Sally Allan and Lilian Mariga.

Further information about videocourses

(*a*) Made in developing countries (N.B. for Pal-B video systems).

Lilian Mariga	Diana Khoo
Zimcare Trust	Cheshire Homes
PO Box BE90	Far Eastern Region
Belvedere	515-Q Jalan Hashim
Harara	11200 Tanjung Bungah
Zimbabwe	Penang, Malaysia

(*b*) Made in Ireland and UK (N.B. for Pal-B video systems).

Sue Jones	Brothers of Charity
St Michael's House	St Aidan's
Upper Kilmacud Road	Gattonside
Stillorgan	Melrose TD6 9NN
Co. Dublin	Scotland
Ireland	

(*c*) Made in USA (N.B. for NTSC Video systems).
Professor Bruce Baker
Department of Psychology,
University of California,
Los Angeles, CA 90024
USA.

156

References

Ager, A. (1990) 'Planning Sustainable Services: Principles for the Effective Targetting of Resources in Developed and Developing Nations', in Fraser, W. I. (Ed.) *Key Issues in Mental Retardation Research*. London: Routledge.

Cullen, C. (1988) 'A Review of Staff Training: The Emperor's Old Clothes', *Irish Journal of Psychology*, **9**, 309–23.

Donaldson, J. and Martinson, M. (1977) 'Modifying Attitudes Toward Physically Disabled Persons, *Exceptional Children*, **43**, 337–41.

McBrien, J. A. and Foxen, T. H. (1987) 'A Pyramid Model of Staff Training in Behavioural Methods: The EDY Project', in Hogg, J. and Mittler, P. (Eds) *Staff Training in Mental Handicap*. London: Croom Helm.

McConkey, R. (1988) 'Educating all Parents: An Approach Based on Video', in Marfo, K. (Ed.) *Parent–child Interaction and Developmental Disabilities: Theory, Research and Intervention*. New York: Praeger.

McConkey, R. (1990) 'Using Video as a Teaching Aid', in Thornburn, M. J. and Marfo, K. (Eds) *Practical Approaches to Childhood Disability in Developing Countries: Insights from Experience and Research*. Available from Kofi Marfo, College of Education, 405 White Hall, Kent State University, Kent, Ohio 44242, USA.

McConkey, R. and Price, P. (1986) *Let's Talk: Learning Language in Everyday Settings*. Dublin: St Michael's House, and London: Souvenir Press.

McConkey, R. and Templer, S. (1987) 'Videocourses for Training Staff in Developing Countries', *International Journal of Rehabilitation Research*, **10**, 206–10.

Thornburn, M. (1990) 'Training Community Workers for Early Detection, Assessment and Intervention', in Thornburn, M. J. and Marfo, K. (Eds) *Practical Approaches to Childhood Disability in Developing Countries: Insights from Experience and Research*. Available from Kofi Marfo, College of Education, 405 White Hall, Kent State University, Kent, Ohio 44242, USA.

Thornburn, M. J. and Roeher, G. A. (1986) 'A Realistic Approach to the Preparation of Personnel for Rehabilitation Services in Developing Countries', in Marfo, K., Walker, S. and Charles, B. (Eds) *Childhood Disability in Developing Countries*. New York: Praeger.

Werner, D. and Bower, B. (1982) *Helping Health Workers Learn*. Palo Alto, CA: Hisparian Foundation.

World Health Organization (1985) *Mental Retardation: Meeting the Challenge*. Geneva: WHO.

CHAPTER 15

Innovations in Special Needs Staff Training in Further Education

David Hutchinson

Introduction

By way of an introduction to this chapter which is about training to meet special needs in further education (post school), I have chosen to examine first the ways in which provision for students with special needs in further education has, itself, grown. The justification for this approach is that what has taken place in the development of provision for students, to some extent, is reflected in the development of training opportunities for further education teachers and, certainly, some of the characteristics evident in the one are also present in the other.

Developing opportunities for students with special needs

In Britain the provision of educational opportunities for students with special needs in further education has had a different and a much more recent history than provision for the same groups of young people at school. Special education in schools has a long history which can be traced back into the nineteenth century, with some significant landmarks along the way, such as the 1944 Education Act and the 1981 Education Act, where attention has been focused upon the need to develop further that provision. This has not been the case post-school and the report 'Handicapped School-Leavers: Their Further Education, Training and Employment' (Tuckey *et al.*, 1973) illustrates the point well in showing that there was a marked difference in the percentage of those young people who were considered to be suitable for post-school education and those who actually received any. This view was confirmed in 1978 by the Warnock Committee which said in its report 'For the great majority of young people with disabilities or significant difficulties the year in which they are 16 marks the end of formal education' (DES, 1978). Many of the people who provided evidence to the Warnock Committee and contributed towards its deliberations expressed very strongly the view that post-school educational opportunities should be available to young people with disabilities and it is, perhaps, for this reason that the Committee suggested that 'provision for young people over 16 with special needs has in our view been badly neglected in the past'. In response, not only did the Committee make several recommendations intended to bring about an improvement in this situation, it also accorded them high status as one of the three areas of first priority.

The post-Warnock period saw a general increase in Local Education Authority provision for young people with special needs in further education colleges. To some extent these developments were fuelled by growing youth unemployment in the late 1970s and the early 1980s but there was, nevertheless, an increasing awareness of the entitlement of young people with special needs to receive post-school education and this added to the demand for places. The report 'Catching Up?' (Stowell, 1987) was based upon a survey of provision for students with special educational needs in further and higher education undertaken by the National Bureau for Handicapped Students (now Skill: The National Bureau for Students with Disabilities) on behalf of the Department of Education and Science. This indicated that in excess of 40,000 students with special needs were attending colleges on a variety of programmes, though not all of them full-time. However, as Bookis (1984) and Bramley and Harris (1986) have shown, provision was not developing universally nor equally and factors such as type of disability and geographical location were responsible for some students having difficulty in obtaining a college place. Such was this pattern of variation that the late Barry Taylor, the then Chief Education Officer for Somerset, suggested in 1985 at a conference organised by the National Bureau for Handicapped Students, that 'Post-16 provision is an area of very serious concern... there are some examples of first class practice surrounded by deserts of nothing... in general terms 16–19 special needs is a most underdeveloped area, good provision is a matter of geographical lottery... where you live, there is no national system'. To some extent this view was reflected in the HMI report 'Students with Special Needs in Further Education' (DES, 1989) which, reflecting upon the fact that the proportion of students with special needs attending college is less than might be expected given the Warnock Committee's estimates of prevalence, says that 'There is scope for more extensive provision and more vigorous marketing of it'. Nevertheless, despite the previous comments, post-school provision for young people and adults with special needs is an embedded feature of the national range of educational opportunity and is likely to remain so for the foreseeable future. This view is reflected in the duty placed upon Local Education Authorities to 'Have regard to the requirements of persons over compulsory school age who have learning difficulties' (para 120 [10] Education Reform Act, 1988).

Developing training opportunities

Up to the publication of the Warnock Report in 1978 it would be fair to say that training to meet special needs in further education was not something which formed part of the recognised agenda of training opportunities. Indeed, I would go as far as suggesting that anyone who did work in this field and who wished to undertake professional development would, until recently, have only been able to do so via the mechanism of courses of training set up to meet the needs of teachers working in schools. Many college staff working with students with special needs in further education colleges did avail themselves of this opportunity and were able to share a useful experience with school-based colleagues. As such they were engaging in a prototype of collaborative working, a theme which will be returned to later.

It would be true to say that the growth in provision for students with special needs has not been matched by an equal increase in staff development opportunities. As indicated above, the Warnock Committee made provision for young people with special needs one of its three areas of first priority. The same report also prioritised teacher training and made a number of recommendations associated with the teaching of students with special needs. Some of these are relevant to the current discussion:

(i) A special education element should be included in all initial training courses for further education teachers . . . short part-time courses which cover the same ground as the special educational element should also be provided (DES, 1978, Para 12.68).

Unlike teachers in schools, further education lecturers do not always have initial teaching qualifications. A policy statement issued by the National Association of Teachers in Further and Higher Education (1978) suggested that 'many of the urgent, specific and long term problems currently facing further and higher education would have been reduced if there had been a systematic pattern of teacher education for this area'. The NATFHE statement reflects the view that at the time two thirds of further education teachers had received no initial teacher education but, additionally, it embodies the belief that there should be a continuous programme of professional development for the teacher in order to be able to meet new challenges, a point which will be returned to in the next section.

As most further education teachers who receive initial training on either a pre-service or an in-service basis do so at a limited number of colleges or polytechnics, it is not a difficult task to review progress in light of the Warnock recommendation. It would be true to say that all of these establishments have addressed the issue of training to meet special needs to a lesser or greater degree, but it would not be true to say that a special educational element is included for all those teachers who are receiving their initial training. It may well be that special needs issues are introduced into Cert. Ed. programmes as a 'bolt-on' but it would be a more accurate reflection of the current situation to say that such an input is available mainly for those who opt for a discrete special needs pathway.

> (ii) Short courses should be provided in particular aspects of the teaching of young people and adults with special needs (DES, 1978, Para 12.71).

It is true that many Local Education Authorities, Regional Advisory Councils for Further Education, the Department of Education and Science, the Further Education Staff College, together with voluntary organisations, especially the National Bureau for Students with Disabilities, have provided short courses of training but these have largely been organised on a 'one-off', ad hoc basis and there appears to have been little consideration of an on-going programme with any logical structure.

Whilst the general response to Warnock's recommendations has been disappointing, there have been a number of interesting and significant developments. One examination body concerned with further education teacher training and staff development, the City and Guilds of London Institute, has given the matter some consideration and has provided a one-year, part-time certificated course entitled

'Teaching Students with Special Needs in Further Education'. This course was launched in 1977/78, coincidentally with the publication of the Warnock Report, and by 1987/88 some 4,000 students had been awarded the certificate. The original course has now been revised, up-dated and re-introduced on a modular basis as the 'Certificate in Continuing Professional Development (Special Needs)'. This modified version is proving equally popular with college staff. Similarly a number of institutes of higher education have either modified their existing special needs programmes of study, such as the Diploma in Professional Studies in Education to make them more relevant to further education teachers or, in the case of others, such as the Cambridge Institute of Education, have introduced specifically designed dedicated programmes. Likewise, the Open University has introduced material concerned with training to meet special needs in further and continuing education into its degree, diploma and pro-fessional development programmes.

In June 1984, the Advisory Committee on the Supply and Education of Teachers (ACSET) produced a report (DES, 1984) on teacher training and special educational needs. The recommendations contained in this report both reiterated and extended those made in the earlier Warnock Report. The ACSET Report led to the establishment by the Department of Education and Science of a further education special needs teacher training working group. The terms of reference of this group were:

   (i) to examine the recommendations for the FE sector made by ACSET in its report of June 1984 on teacher training and special educational needs;

  (ii) to consider how far a basis already exists for the development of an FE system of general awareness training and specialist training to the extent recommended;

 (iii) to suggest how the most effective use may be made of existing resources of staff and materials for these purposes and what developments are desirable to reinforce these resources.

The findings of the working group were published in 1987 under the title 'A "Special" Professionalism' (DES, 1987). The report generally confirmed the ACSET recommendations and made further recommendations concerning both short and long term objectives for training to meet special needs in further education. Without doubt both the ACSET Report and 'A "Special" Professionalism' raised the profile of this area of training and a number of initiatives have stemmed from them at local and national level. Whilst the full impact of the implementation of the latter report has, as yet, to be fully assessed it would be accurate to say that they have had a significant impact in the field and led to the subsequent inclusion of special needs in further education as a priority area in the Local Education Authority Training Grants Scheme. This has inevitably stimulated the provision of training activity across the country.

Special initiatives

However, changes in opportunity such as the ones mentioned above, laudable though they may be, cannot meet the needs of every teacher. Bradley *et al.* (1983) have indicated some staff have had difficulty in obtaining the release necessary to attend courses and others, who only teach students with special needs on a part-time basis as but one part of their general teaching duties, have given low priority to this area within the context of their own development plans. Bradley *et al.*, also refer to the isolation of special needs lecturers who may form very small teams and be submerged in some extremely large and complex colleges. Nevertheless, they note their dedication in terms of participating in whatever staff development activities are on offer, often in their own time and at their own expense, together with the fact that some lecturers have initiated self-help activities designed to share common problems and discuss possible solutions.

An additional difficulty for establishing training to meet special needs lies in the fact that staff development in further education is a relatively new phenomenon which has its origins largely in the mid 1970s, at a time of financial difficulty associated with a decline in the demand for college places. In this situation many staff, at the least, faced reduced promotion prospects if not the grave threat of redundancy. At the same time these same teachers were being asked to develop additional professional skills to meet the needs of what has been described by Bradley *et al.* (1983) as a new student group. This new student group had been created both by the introduction of a range of new courses such as those developed under the initiatives of the Manpower Services Commission in the field of youth and adult training, and by the presence of new groups of students not previously represented in colleges. Included in both of these categories were to be found students with special needs.

Reference has already been made to the policy statement issued by the National Association of Teachers in Further and Higher Education concerning the need for the professional development of college staff.

What was very evident was the real absence of any agreement on the nature of this staff development. This is well illustrated by a statement made by the Further Education Unit (FEU, 1982): 'the range of definitions associated with staff development, further professional study . . . in-service training . . . in-service education, in fact represents wide differences of opinion regarding both the concepts and the processes to be used'. These differences have caused some confusion, if not a little controversy, in the field and have tended to polarise around those who favour either the 'professional' or the 'organisational' model of staff development.

The 'professional' model, as advocated by the James Committee (DES, 1972), saw the purpose of staff development 'to reflect and enhance the status and independence of the teaching profession and of the institutions within which many teachers are educated and trained'. Within this model lies the suggestion that staff development should be orientated towards the needs of individual teachers who would make their choice of programme from the packages laid before them.

The 'organisational' model is based not on the needs of individual teachers but on the needs of institutions in particular and the education system in general. The Further Education Unit (1982) sees this model as attempting 'to rationalise staff development activities for individual teachers within the context of the decisions which have to be made about resources and priorities for action and of the fact that teachers have to work co-operatively in particular institutions to meet the needs of particular groups of learners'.

The debate over the two models of staff development has been contentious and confusing where, for example the two could be seen working side by side in the same college. This has led the Further Education Unit, as the leading body in the field concerned with both staff and curriculum development, to attempt to resolve the confusion by suggesting a curriculum-led model of staff development 'by focusing on that which brings professionals and organisations together, the demands of the curriculum'. This model has at its heart the view that the needs of students determine the curriculum and in turn staff development.

Staff training opportunity for school-based special needs staff has tended to follow traditional patterns and has much of the 'professional' model about it, being largely 'course-based'. The absence of any real opportunity for college staff to follow these traditional patterns has led not only to a high demand for training but also for new methods of training. In light of what has been said thus far, it is not surprising to find that the Further Education Unit has provided the main response to these issues and, because of this, it is also not surprising to find that the real innovations in the field are both student-centred and curriculum-led.

The Further Education Unit was established to be a focal point for the further education curriculum and to develop a more coordinated response to curriculum development. It has done this in a number of significant ways:

(1) by reviewing and evaluating existing curricula;
(2) by determining curriculum priorities;
(3) by initiating curriculum studies, development and evaluation;
(4) by disseminating the results of its work.

Special needs in further education has been designated as an area of priority by the Further Education Unit and since 1981 it has produced an impressive list of publications. More particularly there have been three major pieces of curriculum development:

(a) for students with moderate learning difficulties (FEU, 1984);
(b) for students with severe physical disabilities (Hutchinson and Tennyson, 1986);
(c) for students with severe learning difficulties (Dee, 1988).

Each of these pieces of work has been concerned with curriculum development but as it would be difficult to develop the curriculum without the staff who deliver it, staff development is also an integral feature. Collaboration with other bodies has been a feature of the Further Education Unit's staff development work and is indicated by the following examples:

(i) with the Department of Education and Science and the National Foundation for Educational Research to produce a staff development pack for further education teachers of students with moderate learning difficulties, 'From Coping to Confidence' (DES/FEU/NFER, 1985);
(ii) with the National Bureau for Handicapped Students (now Skill: The National Bureau for Students with Disabilities) to produce 'A College Guide: Meeting Special Educational Needs' (FEU, 1986);
(iii) with the Training Agency and Skill to produce a staff development resource pack for those working with learners who have special needs, 'Learning Support' (Training Agency/FEU/Skill, 1989).

The pathway indicated by the Further Education Unit in curriculum-led staff development to meet special needs in further education has been followed by a number of other bodies. The most notable of these has been Skill: The National Bureau for Students with Disabilities which, in addition to collaborating with other agencies and producing its own impressive list of staff development materials, has established a nationwide network of staff working in the field. This network is regionally based and provides an excellent opportunity for those engaged in the field to provide their own training supported by a national body.

Conclusions

The absence of a coordinated programme of staff development to meet special needs in further education has, without doubt, had its consequences especially in the field of award-bearing programmes. Nevertheless, this very absence of opportunity has created the concept of staff development based upon self help. Within this has been embodied the notion of curriculum-led staff development as advocated by the Further Education Unit. This, together with the establishment of support networks, now evident at national, regional and local level, have been the real innovations in the field.

Recent developments are now indicating further areas for innovation which point up future training needs. Fish (1989) introduces a new definition of special needs based not upon the labelling of the learner in a category of disability but in terms of the listing of support needs. Thus 'special' is defined as the 'special support that certain learners need to succeed in their learning'. As support for students with special needs is provided by a number of agencies it is important that they all work to common aims and objectives. This has implications for staff development, and the notion of inter-agency collaborative training is emerging as an important issue. In a recently published series of papers entitled 'Working Together' (FEU, 1989) based upon work undertaken as part of a United Kingdom contribution to an OECD/CERI project, the Further Education Unit refers to this aspect of training, and this has also been developed at a practical level by Hutchinson (1991) as a follow-up to the Further Education Unit's curriculum framework for students with severe physical disability. There is little doubt that if the needs of students are to be met fully then this type of training will have to be a priority for future training activity.

166

References

Bookis, J. (1984) *Beyond the School Gate*, London: RADAR.

Bradley, J., Chesson, R. and Silverleaf, J. (1983) *Inside Staff Development*. Windsor: NFER-Nelson.

Bramley, K. and Harris, J. (1986) 'Special Needs and FE in Wales', *British Journal of Special Education*, **13**, 1, March.

Dee, L. (1988) *New Directions: A Curriculum Framework for Students with Severe Learning Difficulties*. London: FEU.

Department of Education and Science (1972) *Teacher Education and Training*. (Report of a Committee of Enquiry chaired by Lord James of Rusholme). London: HMSO.

Department of Education and Science (1978) *Special Educational Needs: Report of the Committee of Enquiry into the Education of Handicapped Children and Young People*. (The Warnock Report). London: HMSO.

Department of Education and Science (1984) *Teacher Training and Special Educational Needs: Report of the Advisory Committee on the Supply and Education of Teachers*. London: HMSO.

Department of Education and Science (1987) *A 'Special' Professionalism: Report of the FE Special Needs Teacher Training Working Group*. London: HMSO.

Department of Education and Science (1989) *Education Observed No. 9: Students with Special Needs in Further Education*. London: HMSO.

DES/FEU/NFER (1985) *From Coping to Confidence: A Staff Development Resource Pack for FE Teachers of Students with Moderate Learning Difficulties*. London: DES/FEU/NFER.

Fish, J. (1989) *Descriptions, Definitions and Directions: Special Needs in Further and Continuing Education*. Occasional Paper No. 7. London: FEU/Longmans.

Further Education Unit (1982) *Teacher Skills: Towards a Strategy of Staff Development and Support for Vocational Preparation*. London: FEU.

Further Education Unit (1984) *Skills for Living: A Curriculum Framework for Students with Moderate Learning Difficulties*. London: FEU.

Further Education Unit (1986) *A College Guide: Meeting Special Educational Needs*. London: FEU/Longmans.

Further Education Unit (1989) *Working Together*. London: FEU.

Hutchinson, D. (1991) *Supporting Transition to Adulthood: A Staff Training Package*. London: FEU.

Hutchinson, D. and Tennyson, C. (1986) *Transition to Adulthood: A Curriculum Framework for Students with Severe Physical Disability*. London: FEU.

National Association of Teachers in Further and Higher Education (1978) *The Education and Training of Teachers for Further and Higher Education: A Policy Statement*. London: NATFHE.

Stowell, R. (1987) *Catching Up? Provision for Students with Special Educational Needs in Further and Higher Education*. London: National Bureau for Handicapped Students.

Training Agency/FEU/Skill (1989) *Learning Support: A Staff Development Resource Pack for those Working with Learners with Special Needs.* London: Training Agency/FEU/Skill.

Tuckey, L., Parfitt, J. and Tuckey, B. (1973) *Handicapped School Leavers: Their Further Education, Training and Employment.* Windsor: NFER.

CHAPTER 16

Training Issues in Developing Countries

Venta L. Kabzems

In developing countries innovative frameworks for special education teacher training need to be developed in response to increased demands for services, changes in educational knowledge, changes in service delivery systems and changes in enrolment patterns. While near-universal primary education has been achieved by many developing nations, civil strife in others leaves millions unschooled or restricts their access to educational institutions and, in some countries, rising HIV infection rates are causing changes in enrolment patterns as well as a drop in the number of teaching personnel.

The long-term objective of educational reform in many developing nations has been to eliminate the differences in education between élite and peasant groups. But legislation which sees education as a right and open to all children creates a massive increase in demand for teachers, including specialist teachers, which frequently far outstrips the teacher training system's ability to supply personnel. In addition, reformers have often neglected to consult the service providers (e.g., teachers) or the consumers (students, families, employers) of special educational services in the design of teacher education programmes in spite of the obvious need for conceptualizations of special education in a region to be reflected in the training of teachers and in approaches to service delivery.

If any model of service delivery is to effectively cater for children with special needs, it is important for teachers to be able to put into practice a wide range of instructional interventions for students with mildly handicapping conditions. If anything this is more important in the context of educational development than it is in more developed educational systems. In situations where teachers have access to limited specialist support it is vital that all teachers should be able to address the educational needs of students who suffer from visual and hearing impairments, are gifted/talented, have specific learning disabilities, display evidence of mental retardation, have physical handicaps or experience mild forms of communication disorder. It is not realistic to expect newly trained teachers to know everything about exceptional learners, but it is not unreasonable to expect a teacher education programme to provide a non-categorical approach to the instruction of learners who may require assistive devices or curricula or methodological variations for effective learning. At the same time all teachers should know what additional help is available, how to get it and how to use it for the benefit of their students. In some regions this may mean knowledge of organizations which can provide assistance in the form of written information, in other areas it may be the knowledge of persons involved in community-based rehabilitation, while in others it may be knowledge of the existence and location of specialist facilities within the country.

The effectiveness of highly specialised teacher training programmes intended to meet the needs of students with severe handicapping conditions is not being questioned. However, where statistics are available, it would appear that the majority of exceptional learners are found outside specialised facilities in developing countries. The majority of students with special educational needs are already in integrated settings, even if this is only by default. In order to ensure that these children are taught effectively, regular teacher education programmes need to look at ways to incorporate techniques and methods for working with exceptional learners into their syllabi.

Having said these things it is, however, important to recognise that in developing countries the existence of teacher training programmes, especially those involving any sort of specialist training, are particularly affected by non-educational pressures such as those which stem from the wider economic and political sphere of a nation. Stable funding arrangements are not the norm in many developing countries as political conflict, rising energy costs or a shift in the priorities of a donor agency may have drastic effects on the supply of or demand for educational services.

Candidate selection

It has been suggested that students entering specialist teacher education programmes could be likened to an 'investor entering the market place' (Sears, Marshall and Otis-Wilborn, 1989) in that special education teacher training offers quick entry into an otherwise crowded profession in many developing countries. Specialist certification has 'additional value' in that it can be used to assist in securing an administrative post or a transfer to a more desirable location (Okech, 1989). It can even be 're-invested' in that it can facilitate a move into another career such as personnel management or sales where the financial rewards are greater than in government service. Consequently, care needs to be taken in selecting students lest scarce resources are expended on training personnel who do not repay that investment by remaining within the field.

Entry to teacher education programmes in many parts of the world is based on the results of around ten or eleven years of formal schooling. With the rapid expansion of education in many countries, entry qualifications have been lowered and primary certificated teachers have been deployed as secondary level teachers while untrained personnel have filled the consequent vacancies at the primary level. In this process the area of special education has also suffered, with many poorly qualified personnel having been recruited to fill staffing vacancies. Subsequently when decisions have been made to upgrade the qualifications of such special education teachers, it is often found that they cannot be selected for staff development or regular teacher training programmes because they lack an adequate academic background. The question then remains of what is to be done with these individuals who have demonstrated commitment to the education of exceptional learners, but who do not meet the requirements for entry into teacher education programmes?

The structures which have been adopted for the provision of teacher education in many developing countries also militate against the creation of a highly qualified cadre of special educationists. Teacher certification programmes are often carried out in a teacher's college while degree programmes in education are most often carried out in a university setting subsequent to successful certification at a lower level plus teaching experience. The problem which arises from this situation is that degree programmes are often designed to enhance the qualifications of secondary school teachers and to prepare them for teaching in the upper forms of secondary schools. Special education training is frequently provided at the post-certificate level, but not necessarily at the degree level. It is also difficult for primary-trained teachers to enter university level programmes as they do not have a subject specialism. However, the usual expectation for staff who work in the teachers colleges is that they should have a degree. This clearly militates against special education personnel and primary teachers obtaining posts in teacher education programmes. Thus, special education courses may not be staffed by tutors who are familiar with the practical aspects of primary level classrooms or special education. Such a system also does a disservice to secondary-trained teachers who wish to obtain special education certification, not to mention exceptional learners who require support at the secondary level.

Planning issues

Although governments generally provide the majority of funds for education, in developing countries community involvement and that of foreign donors in supporting the provision of special education is common and is usually welcomed for the financial relief provided. This can, however, create problems for governments agencies, for institutions and for individuals. When funding comes from outside bodies, the agency or person in control of the disbursement of the funds within the government service acquires a great deal of power. People without experience of this situation may have difficulty imagining the incentive quality which access to foreign exchange or the opportunity for foreign travel can have for people working in conditions of economic stringency. Potential for the mismanagement of these funds is great when local salaries are low, foreign exchange restrictions are tight, or the donor agency is perceived as insensitive to the local culture. It is unfortunately the case that innovative programmes of training sometimes do not achieve their aims for reasons such as these. An additional problem which often arises when training programmes are established with the use of external funds is that when the money is exhausted (legitimately or otherwise) the programmes are discontinued because of the lack of government funds for their maintenance.

The provision of special educational training (and special education) is particularly susceptible to economic influences in developing countries. A factor which sometimes inhibits the development of a highly qualified force of special educators in some countries is the fact that if the level of teachers' qualifications rise they become increasingly expensive commodities. The greatest proportion of any education budget goes on teachers' salaries, so it may be seen as expedient for a system to keep the qualifications of the main body of its teaching personnel low. Furthermore, long term educational budgeting in many countries is very difficult and fluctuations in government resources available for education are often in a volatile relationship with unstable political events within the country and with neighbouring countries and subject to unpredictable influences of war, famine, civil disobedience, etc. In such circumstances it is an unfortunate fact of life that competition for scarce resources often results in special education and special educational training being seen as a luxury rather than a priority and its development restricted.

Lack of coordinated and efficient planning, which is characteristic of many developed as well as developing countries, does, however, create particular problems for special education and special educational training in developing countries. Different government ministries frequently have responsibility for various components of the education process or may have shifted responsibilities from time to time. For example, responsibility for pre-school education in Zimbabwe has shifted from the Ministry of Primary and Secondary Education to the Ministry of Women's Affairs and Community Development and back to a restructured Ministry of Education and Culture in a single decade. Equally, responsibility for teacher training frequently does not fall under the same administrative jurisdiction as teacher deployment. This situation presents a barrier to communication concerning desirable competencies for teachers as seen by the consumers of educational services, areas of weakness in pre-service training as seen by programme graduates in the field and links between various educational provisions that will be encountered as the child goes from pre-school to adulthood. Subtle competition and power struggles between Ministries undermine efforts to use limited financial resources to the best advantage for the students concerned.

Low salaries affect the motivation levels of teacher educators. Instruction and marking for large classes, distance supervision for practicum students when transportation is difficult, understaffing in most institutions and few opportunities for staff development are factors which do not bode well for innovative approaches to teacher education nor to the retention of teacher educators in the training institutions.

It is also important to recognise the particular problems which are associated with recruiting and retaining qualified personnel in rural areas in developing countries due to difficulties associated with accommodation, water supply, transportation and other social amenities. This is a problem in many developed educational systems but the situation is exacerbated by the fact that the average salary of an urban primary teacher in a country such as Zimbabwe is several times greater than that paid to a rural teacher (Nhundu, 1989).

Syllabus issues

A frequently occurring issue for any developing educational system is that of the 'imported' curriculum. This is a particular problem in specialist training courses, where a course which has been developed in a totally different educational climate is 'imported' without any adaptations for the local cultural, economic or technological situation (Baine, 1985). This sometimes happens as a carry over from previous colonial or governmental regimes, but the 'imported' curriculum is just as likely to have emanated from the teacher educators themselves. Specialised training received outside the country may have required the person to turn his or her back on the local culture for a few years (credentialism has a price). 'West is best' thinking may result in an uncritical acceptance of a philosophy or methodology which is far removed from one's home background. Upon returning to their own country, the new specialists may be out of touch with what is going on in the schools and be unrealistic about what is appropriate for the training of specialists in their own country. A good example of what can occur when teacher educators are caught up with inappropriate models of training occurs in the fields of visual and hearing impairments. In their own training and as a result of their experience in other countries, teacher educators in these fields have often been exposed to the benefits of high technology which they subsequently manage to obtain for their own institution (so we won't be left behind). This latest technology is presented to the students who then find it irrelevant to their work in areas and schools without access to electricity or piped water.

Methods of teaching in many teacher training institutions in developing countries do not facilitate the development of skills appropriate to the needs of 'special children'. While the prevailing ethos in schools and the norms of teaching (what is expected, acceptable and encouraged by the local community) may not be what staff in training institutions view as desirable, it is often difficult for them to overcome the limitations within which they work and foster the development of 'new' teaching skills in their students. Large classes within teacher training institutions all too often resemble those in the schools themselves with the result that teacher trainees do not experience teaching which is much different to that which they experienced as children. Given the dominance of didactic teaching in many developing education systems, the new specialist teacher may leave the institution ready to employ the only methods he or she has ever known and which are unlikely to bring benefits to exceptional learners. For example, Evans (1986) refers to a student whose goal was to be able to teach without a lesson plan and another who, after initial dismay, was prepared to utilise corporal punishment as expected by the local school culture. Part of this could be ameliorated via adequate practicum supervision. However, the quality of field supervision tends to become eroded as the number of trainees increases. All too often an increase in trainee numbers is not accompanied by a proportional rise in the number of supervisory staff and consequently an already inadequate number of supervisory visits drops even further. The chances that these students will develop a large repertoire of practical skills which may not represent good teaching practice are increased. To compound matters, specialist teachers leave a training institution expected to do more than simply instruct children in classrooms. They may have received as part of their training agricultural extension work, adult literacy courses or the expectation that they will act as a community rehabilitation worker.

Cultural issues

In a developing area, poverty as well as social and political tensions can make the delivery of special educational services a demanding prospect. Working with exceptional learners, especially those with multiple or severely handicapping conditions, remains devalued work. Teaching tends to occur in segregated facilities and the disabilities themselves are still frequently associated with witchcraft or maternal wrongdoing. If teachers are to be effective service deliverers, they must be able to find a place in the local culture taking into account the basic belief system of a community. They must know the traditional chain of command. They need to be sensitive to gender roles and social kinship patterns and to recognise that Western models of child development, child rearing, individual rights and freedoms and special educational practices are not easily transposed (nor should they be). Western practices, at best, might be perceived by the local culture as different, possibly interesting but more likely as unnatural, if they are even perceived at all (Miles, 1989). The local school or community culture may leave the teacher feeling that he or she has little room to exercise professional judgement regarding the learning environment in a classroom.

In such a situation it is all too easy for teachers to feel that their professionalism has been eroded and their skills are undervalued. Their position is not made any easier by the fact that it is common for teachers in such communities to be expected to act as advocate for the community when struggling with the government system in order to obtain prosthetic devices for students or remission of school fees for exceptional learners, at the same time as being, in effect, the voice of local or regional government. Such dilemmas can be particularly problematic for the 'expatriate' specialist for whom too radical or vocal an approach to an issue within a community may be perceived as 'going too far', with potential loss of credibility or even the teaching position.

Meeting the challenge

If specialist teacher education programmes are to prepare personnel to work effectively in local schools, then locally acceptable models of service delivery such as community-based rehabilitation and segregated classroom instruction must be reflected in the training which is provided. Existing services in many developing countries are based on a categorical model of service delivery for the obviously disabled. Physical handicaps, visual impairment and hearing impairment tend to be served first in educational institutions, with mental retardation and those with multiple handicaps lagging further behind. Training programmes for specialist teachers clearly need to reflect the reality of this provision, although one would also hope that those involved in specialist teacher education also see themselves as 'agents of change' and attempt through their own work to introduce innovatory practice into the educational system. The need for highly specialised personnel will not diminish; however, attention does need to be focused on the integration in pre-service training of general and special education as well as on in-service staff development to meet a broader range of special needs. A teacher preparation programme which includes generic as well as specialised information about exceptional learners is clearly essential if teachers are to be adequately prepared for what is the reality of most classrooms in the world today.

Change, however, comes slowly and is rarely easy to achieve. The issues involved in teacher education are inevitably part of much larger national events, and reflect factors such as political structure and stability, the availability of funding and the prevailing educational ideology. These influences exist in developed and developing nations but are perhaps more apparent in the conditions of economic stringency which are faced by educational planners in developing countries. In such circumstances, the priority which is accorded to special education and special educational training is even more crucial in determining the resources which are allocated to it and the forms which it takes.

While it might appear feasible to use the experience generated in one culture to design programmes for use in another, caution needs to be exercised in attempting this. Input from persons knowledgeable in the educational system in the culture concerned is essential to ensure the relevance of the imported experience to local conditions, attitudes and expectations. It is important not to devalue local experience and to recognise the value of the expertise which has been developed by local teachers if the programmes which are developed are to have real long-term value. In many developing educational systems the importance of special educational provision has been recognised and there is evidence of an increasing awareness of the need to provide specialist training and to equip all teachers with the skills needed to recognise and provide for the needs of all children. In this chapter an attempt has been made to identify some of the issues which have affected such developments and which are likely to influence future progress. It is hoped that this will be of value to others who are involved in this work and to those who may in future take part in it.

References

Baine, D. (1985) 'Training Instructional Staff for Special Education in Developing Countries', *TASH Newsletter*, **11**, 7–9.

Evans, H. L., (1986) 'Overcoming the Problems of Learning from Field Experiences in Teacher Education', *Caribbean Journal of Education*, **13**, 205–19.

Miles, M. (1989) 'The Role of Special Education in Information Based Rehabilitation', *International Journal of Special Education*, **4**, 111–18.

Nhundu, T. J. (1989) 'The Financing and Provision of Education in Zimbabwe: Towards Greater Equality?', *Educational Review*, **41**, 243–56.

Okech, J. G. (1989) 'Innovation in a BEd Primary Course', *Journal of Education for Teaching*, **15**, 247–54.

Sears, J. T., Marshall, J. D. and Otis-Wilborn, A. (1989) 'The Political Economy of Teacher Training: Attracting High Ability Persons into Education – A Critique', *Teacher Education Quarterly*, **16**, 5–72.

CHAPTER 17

Towards Effective Schools for All

Mel Ainscow

This chapter provides an explanation of the development of an international teacher education project concerned with meeting special needs in ordinary schools. The project is an exercise in international collaboration involving teachers, administrators and teacher educators in many countries.

The focus of this chapter is on the rationale that guides the development of the project. I will explain how this rationale has influenced the major elements of the initiative. These are: its approach to special needs, its style of teacher education, and the model for its dissemination and evaluation. Underpinning the rationale is a particular way of looking at human behaviour that is very different to the perspectives that have traditionally dominated the field of special education. This view, described by some as a 'new paradigm' (e.g., Heshusius, 1989; Iano, 1986; Lincoln and Guba, 1985; Reason, 1988), emphasises the following assumptions:

(1)   Human behaviour can only be understood with respect to particular contexts;
(2)   this understanding can only be achieved by a consideration of these contexts as 'wholes';
(3)   events that occur in these contexts are assumed to be constructed in the minds of participants and can, therefore, only be understood by taking account of these multiple perspectives.

Before considering how this perspective and these assumptions have influenced the rationale of the project I will provide a summary of its development.

The development of the project

The initiative grew out of Unesco's continuing work in encouraging member countries to develop strategies for responding to children's special needs in ordinary schools. A detailed account of the development of the project is provided in Ainscow (1990). A survey of fourteen countries, commissioned by Unesco and carried out by a research team from the University of London (Bowman, 1986), identified three major priorities for policy development. These were:

(1) The provision of compulsory education for all children in the population;
(2) the integration of pupils with disabilities into ordinary schools; and
(3) the upgrading of teacher training as a means of achieving the first two priorities.

The findings of this survey were used as the basis of a series of regional workshops. An outcome of these events was that Unesco was urged to assist in the dissemination of teacher training materials that could be used to facilitate improvements with respect to meeting special needs in ordinary schools. It was also recommended that in carrying out this work, the following points should be kept in mind:

(1) The need to develop national policies for teacher education that progress in a continuous fashion from the pre-service stage through to the in-service stage.
(2) The importance of supervised practical experience as a major element of teacher education programmes.
(3) The importance of taking account of what has been referred to as the 'hidden population' of pupils with special needs. These are children who do not have significant disabilities but who nevertheless experience difficulties in learning. (The original survey, for example, indicated that up to 45 per cent of pupils repeated one or more grades in some countries).
(4) A necessity to increase flexibility of curriculum practice and teaching methods in mainstream classrooms in order to be more responsive to the needs of individual children.
(5) The principle of self-help brought about by encouraging teachers to develop skills of self-evaluation as a means of developing their practice.
(6) The importance of recognising the value of collaboration amongst groups of teachers within a school.
(7) The need to help and encourage teachers to make better use of three sources of non-professional help in the classroom: the pupils themselves, the parents, relatives and others in the community, and paid ancillary help or teachers' aides.

The regional workshops also generated some more specific recommendations regarding the possible content of teacher education programmes.

Consequently, in 1988 I was invited to direct a project to be called 'Special Needs in the Classroom', that would aim to develop and disseminate a resource pack of teacher education materials. A pilot version of the pack is currently being field-tested in eight countries (Canada, Chile, India, Jordan, Kenya, Malta, Spain and Zimbabwe). The materials are intended to be used as part of pre-service or in-service courses.

Clearly the design of suitable teacher education materials represents an enormous challenge. In particular there is the issue of how to produce a pack that can take account of such a wide range of national contexts, especially those in developing countries. This being the case, a number of measures were taken during the formulation of the materials in an attempt to achieve a level of flexibility that could take account of diverse settings. These were as follows:

- a pilot workshop for teachers and teacher educators from various African countries was held in Nairobi, Kenya in April 1989. This allowed various materials and approaches to be evaluated;
- a series of advisory teams consisting of teacher educators and teachers were created in different parts of the world. These teams provided comment on draft materials and contributed materials of their own for inclusion in the pack;
- in addition, a number of special educators around the world read and commented upon the draft materials.

It is as a result of all of these consultation processes that the rationale for the whole project has emerged. The rest of the chapter concentrates on this topic.

Special needs in education

Central to the ways in which educational difficulties have traditionally been conceptualised is the view that they arise because of the limitations and/or disabilities of particular pupils. In other words, certain children are perceived as having things wrong with them that make it difficult for them to participate in the normal curriculum of schools (Bogdan and Kugelmass, 1984; Mercer, 1973).

Three main approaches have resulted from this viewpoint. Current provision in many countries tends to consist of an amalgam of these approaches. They are as follows:

(1) *The withdrawal approach*

Here those pupils who it is felt will not cope with the demands of the mainstream curriculum are withdrawn for at least part of the time to a special class or school. The aim is to provide learning experiences that are more appropriate in that they take account of the limitations of the pupils.

(2) *The remedial approach*

This term is unfashionable these days but the approach it implies is still evident in many schools. It can take a number of forms and involve a variety of strategies. Essentially it attempts to provide forms of intervention that will overcome or compensate for deficits within children.

(3) *The mainstreaming approach*

In this approach the main emphasis is on making modifications in the curriculum to allow access for children regarded as being exceptional. It may, for example, involve the provision of an individualised learning programme, the adaptation of classroom materials, or additional adult support for the child.

It is important to note that despite the differences between these three approaches they each continue to perceive the problem as being the child's. As a result, they exclude from consideration causal factors that may lie in larger social, political and organisational processes that are external to the individual (Skrtic, 1987). Furthermore, the curriculum of ordinary schools remains broadly the same since it is assumed to be appropriate for the great majority of children. The provision of various forms of special education confirms that problems arise because some children are special. In so doing this helps to maintain the status quo of schooling.

There are a number of negative outcomes that can arise from this dominant perspective and these have been well documented (e.g., Ainscow, 1989; Algozzine, 1977; Apter, 1982; Booth, 1988; Hobbs, 1975; Mercer, 1973; Rhodes, 1970; Schrag and Divorky, 1975; Swap, 1978). In summary, the evidence suggests that these traditional approaches work to the disadvantage of the pupils involved in the following ways:

(i) The segregation process and inevitable labelling with which it is associated has negative effects upon the attitudes and expectations of pupils, teachers and parents.

(ii) The presence of designated specialists encourages teachers to pass on to others responsibility for children they regard as being special.

(iii) Resources that might otherwise be used to provide more flexible and responsive forms of schooling are channelled into separate provision.
(iv) The nature of the educational experiences provided is often characterised by narrowness of opportunity.

The more positive orientation that has been adopted in this project is to assume that when children experience significant difficulties in schools that they arise as a result of the *interaction* of a complex range of factors within a given context. In practice the problem is a curriculum one. What we are witnessing is the inability of a teacher or group of teachers to provide classroom experiences that are meaningful and relevant given the interests, experiences, and existing skills and knowledge of particular children (Ainscow and Tweddle, 1988). In making this statement it should not be assumed that I am seeking to replace 'child blaming' with 'teacher blaming' (Reynolds, 1988). It has to be recognised that the capacity of teachers to provide appropriate learning opportunities for their pupils is constrained by wider school structures and systems (Bottery, 1988; Gitlin, 1987), some of which may be imposed from outside the school (Hartnett and Naish, 1990).

In attempting to conceptualise educational difficulty in a more positive way, therefore, we can more usefully see pupils experiencing difficulty as indicators of the need for reform. They point to the need to improve schooling in ways that will enable them to achieve success. It is worth adding at this stage that such reforms are seen as being to the benefit of all pupils. The aim is *effective schools for all*. This approach is consistent with the view expressed by Seamus Hegarty as a result of a review of the current situation in 58 countries (Unesco, 1988). He argued:

> For real progress... integration has to be seen in terms of school reform, whose goal is the creation of a common school offering differentiated provision for all according to need within a single coherent curriculum framework.

In the light of this line of argument the 'Special Needs in the Classroom' project is attempting to help teachers in ordinary schools to be more responsive to all the children in their classes. Consequently, the concern is not with finding technical solutions to the problems of particular children, but with a curriculum challenge that should be shared by all teachers in every school.

Teacher education

How then can this be achieved? How can teachers and others involved in schools be helped to meet the needs of all children in their classes? The rationale of the Unesco project is to argue that one way forward is to encourage teachers to take a more positive approach by learning how to investigate and develop their own classroom practice. The aims are to facilitate understanding and to encourage professional development. This approach is based upon the view that there exist *three* sources that can facilitate improvements in teaching. These are:

(1) *Personal experience*
Arguably the most significant way in which teachers can develop their expertise is by reflecting upon their own experience (Schon, 1983). Consequently the material in the Resource Pack encourages teachers to examine their own practice, formulate priorities for development and take responsibility for making improvements.

(2) *Colleagues*
Too often teachers work in professional isolation. There is, however, considerable evidence to show that collaboration with colleagues can be a powerful means of enhancing professional development (e.g., Joyce and Showers, 1988). Throughout the materials, therefore, strategies are provided that will encourage teachers to cooperate with one another in developing their practice.

(3) *Research evidence*
Traditionally teacher education has tended to be concerned with the passing on of theories derived from research as a means of bringing about improvements in classroom practice. The materials in the Resource Pack include ideas drawn from research but these are seen as a means of supporting teacher development, *not* as the only source of improvement. Personal experience and collaboration with colleagues are regarded as the central sources for the professional development of teachers.

Consequently the 'Special Needs in the Classroom' materials incorporate new perspectives on special education into a pack that also takes note of trends in teacher education. Furthermore, the assumption is made that those using the pack, course leaders and participants, will be seen as contributing to a process of collaborative inquiry as to how classrooms can be made more responsible to the needs of individual pupils.

The overall *aim* of the pack is as follows:

To help teachers to develop their thinking and practice with respect to the ways in which they respond to pupils' special educational needs.

There is considerable evidence to indicate that programmes of staff development can help to facilitate developments in professional practice provided they are well planned and based on sound principles (e.g., Ainscow and Muncey, 1989; Browdler, 1983; Joyce and Showers, 1988; Loucks-Horsley *et al.*, 1987; Powers, 1983). From an analysis of these and other sources, it was decided that the resource pack should emphasise the following *strategies*:

(1) *Active learning*
Active approaches to problem solving, with a particular emphasis on group work, as opposed to the didactic teaching style of so much teacher education in the past, encourages participation and seems to overcome fear of change (Fullan, 1982; Houston and Frieberg, 1979; Muncey and Ainscow, 1986; Powers, 1983).

(2) *Negotiation of objectives*
Involvement of participants in the negotiation of their own learning objectives within the overall framework of a course, facilitates a commitment to new approaches and provides a means of taking account of varied needs (Cruickshank *et al.*, 1979; McLoughlin, 1976; Powers, 1983).

(3) *Demonstration, practice and feedback*
Joyce and Showers (1988) argue that implementation of new ideas or new ways of working is most likely when these three elements are used collectively. Demonstrations may take place in settings that simulate the workplace, mediated through film or video, or conducted live in the classroom. As far as practice is concerned, the closer the training setting approximates the teacher's usual workplace the more transfer is facilitated. At this stage 'peer teaching' (practice alongside other teachers) is helpful. Feedback can also be provided when teachers work together cooperatively, using what Joyce and Showers refer to as 'peer coaching'.

(4) *Continuous evaluation*
The active involvement of course participants in monitoring their own learning can also enhance motivation (Powers, 1983). The aim should be to encourage teachers to see themselves as learners, learning alongside their pupils in the classroom, and becoming what Schon (1983) has called 'reflective practitioners'. Continuous evaluation is also important as a means of influencing the development of course

activities and priorities in response to the needs of individual participants.

(5) *Support*

In addition, the importance of long-term support for teachers seeking to develop their practice cannot be overstated if new approaches are to be fully implemented (Fullan, 1982, 1985; Hopkins, 1986; Ruddock, 1981).

It is important to understand that the materials and activities in the pack encourage course leaders to model at the adult level effective strategies for meeting individual needs within a class of learners. In other words the features of the pack that are seen as facilitating adult learning within course sessions are intended to be used as a basis for working with children in school.

Dissemination and evaluation

At this stage of the initiative the limited dissemination that is taking place is part of the development process for the project materials. In April 1990 two coordinators from each of the eight countries referred to earlier took part in a workshop/seminar held at the University of Zimbabwe. The first week of this took the form of a demonstration workshop in which I used materials from the Resource Pack to conduct a series of course sessions for the coordinators and a further group of local teachers and student teachers. In the second week the demonstration workshop was evaluated as the basis of a seminar in which the international coordinators planned together the ways in which they would field-test the resource pack in their own countries.

At the time of writing this chapter the field-testing is underway in each of the eight countries. The nature of this work varies from place to place. In some countries the emphasis is on work in initial training courses; in others the materials are being used to organise workshops for groups of teachers taken out of school; and in some cases the initiative is being seen as a school-based review and development process.

The aim of this field-testing is to gather information that can be used to inform the further development of the Resource Pack and its future dissemination. Consequently, the 16 coordinators are seen as members of an international resource team collaborating in the design and promotion of the project. It is intended that they will assist with the wider dissemination process at a later stage.

In terms of evaluation, the central question that is to be addressed is,

'How can the Resource Pack be developed and disseminated in a way that will be appropriate for teachers in different countries?'.

The coordinators in each country will prepare a report in 1991 about their work on the project. The aim is that each report should explain in detail what happened as the resource materials were used in a particular context and what has been learned from the experience. In order to be consistent with the whole rationale of the initiative the reports must include interpretations of these events from the perspectives of *all* participants. Of particular interest will be the ways in which the materials and ideas in the pack relate to the social, cultural and educational traditions of each country (Miles, 1989).

Whilst the emphasis is on providing accounts that make sense of what happened in each context there is also a need to make comparisons between the experience in different countries. Consequently, a common framework has been agreed amongst the team of coordinators that should help in leading to evaluation reports that will have a common pattern. This framework consists of a series of evaluation questions addressed to course leaders and participants related to the following aspects of the field-testing:

Implementation	–	the use of the materials in the resource pack within teacher education contexts.
Process	–	interactions that are based upon the materials associated with the resource pack.
Content	–	the format of the resource pack including the various written materials.
Outcomes	–	changes of attitude, thinking or practice thought to have occurred as a result of the use of the resource pack.

Data that can be used to address the evaluation questions are being collected by the following procedures:

(1) *Course journal*

This is simply a diary in which coordinators and others who may act as course leaders write their thoughts, comments and reflections on the running of each course session. It will have two types of information: factual notes about what occurred, and interpretative comments. Consequently, its content should be helpful in the process of planning course sessions. At a later stage those who read the evaluation reports will also be able to consider the content of the journal in order to have a better understanding of what happened during the field-testing. Where there is more than one leader for a particular course they each keep separate journals.

(2) *Group reports*

Towards the end of a course and, where appropriate, at key stages within a longer course, participants are asked to work in small groups to prepare a written report. They are given a list of questions and asked to consider which of these seem to be relevant to their considerations. They are also requested to make comments on any other significant issues that they believe to be important. These reports should be written in a form that will be accessible to a wider audience.

(3) *Participants' questionnaires*

These are completed anonymously by all individual participants *after* the group reports have been completed. The aim is to provide individuals with an opportunity to give their private views on aspects of the course. It is also intended that these group discussions should be useful in helping participants to formulate their ideas.

In completing their evaluation reports the coordinators are asked to take care in establishing the trustworthiness of their findings. In particular they have been asked to collaborate with their colleagues, including participants, in order to verify their interpretations. Throughout, the emphasis is therefore on taking account of multiple perspectives. Wherever possible, follow-up visits are being made to evaluate the longer-term impact upon thinking and practice.

Conclusion

Even at a superficial level the project described in this chapter is an impressive one. Whilst there is much to do and much to be learned, the project has already had some considerable success in bringing together people from many countries and cultures to share in a common mission.

Perhaps even more significant is the attempt the project is making to apply a new perspective to the improvement of practice in education. Traditionally, special education has been perceived as a technical task in which teachers are introduced to strategies derived from research that are intended to solve the problems of individual children (Iano, 1986). I have argued elsewhere that this narrow perspective has had the effect of limiting opportunities for improving practice (Ainscow, 1989). Consequently, this project is seeking to adopt a more open, holistic perspective to the improvement of teaching. This means that the ways in which individuals interact with and make sense of particular contexts is seen as being vital to understanding and development. Furthermore, this perspective guides the way in which educational difficulties are conceptualised, the way teachers are helped to improve their practice and, indeed, the way the project involves all participants in a process of collaborative inquiry and development. The aim is to find ways of making schools into places where pupils *and* teachers can take responsibility for their own learning.

References

Ainscow, M. (1989) (Ed.) *Special Education in Change.* London: David Fulton Publishers.

Ainscow, M. (1990) 'Special Needs in the Classroom: The Development of a Teacher Education Resource Pack,' *International Journal of Special Education*, **5**, 1, 13–20.

Ainscow, M. and Muncey, J. (1989) *Meeting Individual Needs in the Primary School.* London: David Fulton Publishers.

Ainscow, M. and Tweddle, D. A. (1988) *Encouraging Classroom Success.* London: David Fulton Publishers.

Algozzine, B. (1977) 'The Emotionally Disturbed Child: Disturbed or Disturbing?', *Journal of Abnormal Child Psychology*, **5**, 2, 205–11.

Apter, S. J. (1982) *Troubled Children, Troubled Systems.* New York: Pergamon.

Bogdan, R. and Kugelmass, J. (1984) 'Case Studies of Mainstreaming: A Symbolic Interactionist Approach to Special Schooling', in Barton, L. and Tomlinson, S. (Eds) *Special Education and Social Interests.* London: Croom Helm.

Booth, T. (1988) 'Challenging Conceptions of Integration', in Barton, L. (Ed.) *The Politics of Special Educational Needs.* London: Falmer Press.

Bottery, M. P. (1988) 'Educational Management: An Ethical Critique', *Oxford Review of Education*, **14**, 3.

Bowman, I. (1986) 'Teacher Training and the Integration of Handicapped Pupils: Some Findings from a Fourteen Nation UNESCO study', *European Journal of Special Needs Education*, **1**, 29–38.

Browdler, D. (1983) 'Guidelines for Inservice Planning', *Exceptional Children*, **49**, 300–306.

Cruickshank, D. R. Lorish, C. and Thompson, L. (1979) 'What We Think We Know About Inservice Education', *Journal of Teacher Education*, **30**, 27–32.

Fullan, M. (1982) *The Meaning of Educational Change.* New York: Teachers College Press.

Fullan, M. (1985) 'Change Processes and the Strategies at the Local Level'. *The Elementary School Journal*, **85**, 3, 391–420.

Gitlin, A. D. (1987) 'Common School Structures and Teacher Behaviour', in Smythe, J. (Ed.) *Educating Teachers: Changing the Nature of Pedagogical Knowledge*, London: Falmer Press.

Hartnett, A. and Naish, M. (1990) 'The Sleep of Reason Breeds Monsters: The Birth of a Statutory Curriculum in England and Wales', *Journal of Curriculum Studies*, **22**, 1, 1–16.

Heshusius, L. (1989) 'The Newtonian Mechanistic Paradigm, Special Education, and Contours of Alternatives: An Overview', *Journal of Learning Disabilities*, **22**, 7, 403–21.

Hobbs, N. (1975) *The Futures of Children: Categories, Labels and their Consequences*. San Francisco: Jossey-Bass.

Hopkins, D. (1986) 'The Change Process and Leadership in Schools', *School Organisation*, **6**, 1, 116–26.

Houston, W. R. and Freiberg, H. J. (1979) 'Perceptual Motion, Blindman's Bluff and Inservice Education', *Journal of Teacher Education*, **30**, 7–9.

Iano, R. P. (1986) 'The Study and Development of Teaching: With Implications for the Advancement of Special Education', *Remedial and Special Education*, **7**, 5, 50–61.

Joyce, B. and Showers, B. (1988) *Student Achievement Through Staff Development*. London: Longman.

Lincoln, Y. S. and Guba, E. G. (1985) *Naturalistic Inquiry*. Beverley Hills: Sage.

Loucks-Horsley, S. *et al.* (1987) *Continuing to Learn: A Guidebook for Teacher Development*. Andover, Mass.: Regional Laboratory for Education Improvement for the Northeast and Islands.

McLoughlin, M. W. (1976) 'Implementation as Mutual Adaptation: Change in Classroom Organisation', *Teachers' College Record*, **77**, 339–51.

Mercer, J. (1973) *Labeling the Mentally Retarded*. Berkeley: University of California Press.

Miles, M. (1989) 'The Role of Special Education in Information Based Rehabilitation', *International Journal of Special Education*, **4**, 2, 111–18.

Muncey, J. and Ainscow, M. (1986) 'Meeting Special Needs in Mainstream Schools: A Translantic Perspective', *International Journal of Special Education*, **1**, 2, 161–76.

Powers, D. A. (1983) 'Mainstreaming and the Inservice Education of Teachers', *Exceptional Children*, **49**, 432–9.

Reason, P. (1988) (Ed.) *Human Inquiry in Action*. Beverley Hills: Sage.

Reynolds, M. C. (1988) 'A Reaction to the JLD Special Series on the Regular Education Initiative', *Journal of Learning Disabilities*, **21**, 6, 352–6.

Ruddock, J. (1981) *Making the Most of the Short Inservice Course*. London: Schools' Council.

Rhodes, W. C. (1970) 'A Community Participation Analysis of Emotional Disturbance', *Exceptional Children*, **36**, 306–14.

Schrag, P. and Divorky, D. (1975) *The Myth of the Hyperactive Child*. New York: Pantheon.

Schon, D. (1983) *The Reflective Practitioner*. New York: Basic Books.

Skrtic, T. M. (1987) 'An Organisational Analysis of Special Education Reform', *Counterpoint*, **8**, 2, 15–19.

Swap, S. (1978) 'The Ecological Model of Emotional Disturbance in Children: A Status Report and Proposed Synthesis', *Behavioural Disorders*, **3**, 3, 156–86.

Unesco (1988) *Review of the Present Situation of Special Education*. Paris: Unesco.